The Lover of Horses

Tess Gallagher is a poet, essayist and short-story writer. She grew up in the logging camps of Olympic Peninsula, Washington State, where she continues to live for most of each year in the town where she was born, Port Angeles. For the rest of the year, she is a professor at Syracuse University. She also holds the Mackey chair for writing at Beloit University. She was the companion and wife of Raymond Carver; and until his death in 1988, they were one of the most celebrated literary couples in America. She has written four books of poetry, a book of essays and was a consultant on a BBC film about the life and work of Raymond Carver. He encouraged her to write *The Lover of Horses*, but the inspiration for the stories came from a mixture of her mother, Georgia Morris's storytelling, and Gallagher's Irish ancestry.

Tess Gallagher

THE LOVER OF HORSES

and other stories

Minerva

A Minerva Paperback

THE LOVER OF HORSES

First published in Great Britain 1989
by Hamish Hamilton Ltd
This Minerva edition published 1990
by Mandarin Paperbacks
Michelin House, 81 Fulham Road, London SW3 6RB

Minerva is an imprint of the Octopus Publishing Group

Copyright © Tess Gallagher 1982, 1983, 1984, 1985, 1986

Some of the stories in this collection originally appeared,
in somewhat different form, in the following publications.
Antaeus ("Turpentine"), *Boulevard* ("Desperate Measures"),
The Missouri Review ("At Mercy"), *The North American Review*
("Beneficiaries"), *Ploughshares* ("Bad Company" and "A Pair of Glasses"),
Syracuse Scholar ("The Woman Who Saved Jesse James"),
Tendril ("Recourse"), and *Zyzzva* ("The Lover of Horses").

"King Death" first appeared in *The New Yorker*
under the title "A Figure of Speech."

"The Wimp" was a winner of the PEN Syndicated Fiction Awards for 1985.

A CIP catalogue record for this title
is available from the British Library

ISBN 0 7493 9027 1

Printed in Great Britain
by Cox and Wyman Ltd, Reading, Berks.

for Ray

Contents

The Lover of Horses

THEY SAY MY GREAT-GRANDFATHER WAS A GYPSY, but the most popular explanation for his behavior was that he was a drunk. How else could the women have kept up the scourge of his memory all these years, had they not had the usual malady of our family to blame? Probably he was both, a gypsy and a drunk.

Still, I have reason to believe the gypsy in him had more to do with the turn his life took than his drinking. I used to argue with my mother about this, even though most of the information I have about my great-grandfather came from my mother, who got it from her mother. A drunk, I kept telling her, would have had no initiative. He would simply have gone down with his failures and

1

had nothing to show for it. But my great-grandfather had eleven children, surely a sign of industry, and he was a lover of horses. He had so many horses he was what people called "horse poor."

I did not learn, until I traveled to where my family originated at Collenamore in the west of Ireland, that my great-grandfather had most likely been a "whisperer," a breed of men among the gypsies who were said to possess the power of talking sense into horses. These men had no fear of even the most malicious and dangerous horses. In fact, they would often take the wild animal into a closed stall in order to perform their skills.

Whether a certain intimacy was needed or whether the whisperers simply wanted to protect their secret conversations with horses is not known. One thing was certain —that such men gained power over horses by whispering. What they whispered no one knew. But the effectiveness of their methods was renowned, and anyone for counties around who had an unruly horse could send for a whisperer and be sure that the horse would take to heart whatever was said and reform his behavior from that day forth.

By all accounts, my great-grandfather was like a huge stallion himself, and when he went into a field where a herd of horses was grazing, the horses would suddenly lift their heads and call to him. Then his bearded mouth would move, and though he was making sounds that could have been words, which no horse would have had reason to understand, the horses would want to hear; and one by one they would move toward him across the open space of the field. He could turn his back and walk down the road, and they would follow him. He was probably drunk my mother said, because he was swaying and mumbling all the while. Sometimes he would stop dead-still in the road and the horses would press up against him and raise and lower their heads as he moved his lips. But because these things were only seen from a distance, and because they have eroded in the telling, it is now impossible to know whether my great-grandfather said anything of importance to the horses. Or even if it was his whispering that had brought about their good behavior. Nor was it clear, when he left them in some barnyard as suddenly as he'd come to them, whether they had arrived at some new understanding of the difficult and complex relationship between men and horses.

Only the aberrations of my great-grandfather's relationship with horses have survived—as when he would bathe in the river with his favorite horse or when, as my grandmother told my mother, he insisted on conceiving his ninth child in the stall of a bay mare named Redwing. Not until I was grown and going through the family Bible did I discover that my grandmother had been this ninth child, and so must have known something about the matter.

These oddities in behavior lead me to believe that when my great-grandfather, at the age of fifty-two, abandoned his wife and family to join a circus that was passing through the area, it was not simply drunken bravado, nor even the understandable wish to escape family obligations. I believe the gypsy in him finally got the upper hand, and it led to such a remarkable happening that no one in the family has so far been willing to admit it: not the obvious transgression—that he had run away to join the circus—but that he was in all likelihood a man who had been stolen by a horse.

This is not an easy view to sustain in the society we live in. But I have not come to it frivolously, and have some basis for my belief. For although I have heard the story of my great-grandfather's defection time and again since childhood, the one image which prevails in all versions is that of a dappled gray stallion that had been trained to dance a variation of the mazurka. So impressive was this animal that he mesmerized crowds with his sliding step-and-hop to the side through the complicated figures of the dance, which he performed, not in the way of Lippizaners—with other horses and their riders—but riderless and with the men of the circus company as his partners.

It is known that my great-grandfather became one of these dancers. After that he was reputed, in my mother's words, to have gone "completely to ruin." The fact that he walked from the house with only the clothes on his back, leaving behind his own beloved horses (twenty-nine of them to be exact), further supports my idea that a powerful force must have held sway over him, something more profound than the miseries of drink or the harsh imaginings of his abandoned wife.

Not even the fact that seven years later he returned and knocked on his wife's door, asking to be taken back, could exonerate him from what he had done, even though his wife did take him in and looked after him until he died some years later. But the detail that no one takes note of in the account is that when my great-grandfather returned, he was carrying a saddle blanket and the black plumes from the headgear of one of the circus horses. This passes by even my mother as simply a sign of the ridiculousness of my great-grandfather's plight—for after all, he was homeless and heading for old age as a "good for nothing drunk" and a "fool for horses."

No one has bothered to conjecture what these curious emblems—saddle blanket and plumes—must have meant to my great-grandfather. But he hung them over the foot of his bed—"like a fool," my mother said. And sometimes when he got very drunk he would take up the blanket and, wrapping it like a shawl over his shoulders, he would grasp the plumes. Then he would dance the mazurka. He did not dance in the living room but took himself out into the field, where the horses stood at attention and watched as if suddenly experiencing the smell of the sea or a change of wind in the valley. "Drunks don't care what they do," my mother would say as she finished her story about my great-grandfather. "Talking to a drunk is like talking to a stump."

Ever since my great-grandfather's outbreaks of gypsy-necessity, members of my family have been stolen by things—by mad ambitions, by musical instruments, by otherwise harmless pursuits from mushroom hunting to childbearing or, as was my father's case, by the more easily recognized and popular obsession with card playing. To some extent, I still think it was failure of imagination in this respect that brought about his diminished prospects in the life of our family.

But even my mother had been powerless against the attraction of a man so convincingly driven. When she met him at a birthday dance held at the country house of one of her young friends, she asked him what he did for a living. My father pointed to a deck of cards in his shirt pocket and said, "I play cards." But love is such as it is, and although my mother was otherwise a deadly practical woman, it seemed she could fall in love with no man but my father.

So it is possible that the propensity to be stolen is somewhat contagious when ordinary people come into contact with people such as my father. Though my mother loved him at the time of the marriage, she soon began to behave as if she had been stolen from a more fruitful and upright life which she was always imagining might have been hers.

My father's card playing was accompanied, to no one's surprise, by bouts of drinking. The only thing that may have saved our family from a life of poverty was the fact that my father seldom gambled with money. Such were his charm and powers of persuasion that he was able to

convince other players to accept his notes on everything
from the fish he intended to catch next season to the sale
of his daughter's hair.

I know about this last wager because I remember the
day he came to me with a pair of scissors and said it was
time to cut my hair. Two snips and it was done. I cannot
forget the way he wept onto the backs of his hands and
held the braids together like a broken noose from which
a life had suddenly slipped. I was thirteen at the time and
my hair had never been cut. It was his pride and joy that
I had such hair. But for me it was only a burdensome
difference between me and my classmates, so I was glad
to be rid of it. What anyone else could have wanted with
my long shiny braids is still a mystery to me.

When my father was seventy-three he fell ill and the
doctors gave him only a few weeks to live. My father was
convinced that his illness had come on him because he'd
hit a particularly bad losing streak at cards. He had lost
heavily the previous month, and items of value, mostly
belonging to my mother, had disappeared from the house.
He developed the strange idea that if he could win at cards
he could cheat the prediction of the doctors and live at
least into his eighties.

By this time I had moved away from home and made
a life for myself in an attempt to follow the reasonable
dictates of my mother, who had counseled her children
severely against all manner of rash ambition and foolhar-
diness. Her entreaties were leveled especially in my direc-
tion since I had shown a suspect enthusiasm for a certain
pony at around the age of five. And it is true I felt I had
lost a dear friend when my mother saw to it that the
neighbors who owned this pony moved it to pasture else-
where.

But there were other signs that I might wander off into
unpredictable pursuits. The most telling of these was that

I refused to speak aloud to anyone until the age of eleven. I whispered everything, as if my mind were a repository of secrets which could only be divulged in this intimate manner. If anyone asked me a question, I was always polite about answering, but I had to do it by putting my mouth near the head of my inquisitor and using only my breath and lips to make my reply.

My teachers put my whispering down to shyness and made special accommodations for me. When it came time for recitations I would accompany the teacher into the cloakroom and there whisper to her the memorized verses or the speech I was to have prepared. God knows, I might have continued on like this into the present if my mother hadn't plotted with some neighborhood boys to put burrs into my long hair. She knew by other signs that I had a terrible temper, and she was counting on that to deliver me into the world where people shouted and railed at one another and talked in an audible fashion about things both common and sacred.

When the boys shut me into a shed, according to plan, there was nothing for me to do but to cry out for help and to curse them in a torrent of words I had only heard used by adults. When my mother heard this she rejoiced, thinking that at last she had broken the treacherous hold of the past over me, of my great-grandfather's gypsy blood and the fear that against all her efforts I might be stolen away, as she had been, and as my father had, by some as yet unforeseen predilection. Had I not already experienced the consequences of such a life in our household, I doubt she would have been successful, but the advantages of an ordinary existence among people of a less volatile nature had begun to appeal to me.

It was strange, then, that after all the care my mother had taken for me in this regard, when my father's illness came on him, my mother brought her appeal to me. "Can you do something?" she wrote, in her cramped, left-handed scrawl. "He's been drinking and playing cards for three days and nights. I am at my wit's end. Come home at once."

Somehow I knew this was a message addressed to the very part of me that most baffled and frightened my mother—the part that belonged exclusively to my father and his family's inexplicable manias.

When I arrived home my father was not there.

"He's at the tavern. In the back room," my mother said. "He hasn't eaten for days. And if he's slept, he hasn't done it here."

I made up a strong broth, and as I poured the steaming liquid into a Thermos I heard myself utter syllables and other vestiges of language which I could not reproduce if I wanted to. "What do you mean by that?" my mother demanded, as if a demon had leapt out of me. "What did you say?" I didn't—I couldn't—answer her. But suddenly I felt that an unsuspected network of sympathies and distant connections had begun to reveal itself to me in my father's behalf.

There is a saying that when lovers have need of moonlight, it is there. So it seemed, as I made my way through the deserted town toward the tavern and card room, that all nature had been given notice of my father's predicament, and that the response I was waiting for would not be far off.

But when I arrived at the tavern and had talked my way past the barman and into the card room itself, I saw that my father had an enormous pile of blue chips at his elbow. Several players had fallen out to watch, heavy-lidded and smoking their cigarettes like weary gangsters. Others were slumped on folding chairs near the coffee urn with its empty "Pay Here" styrofoam cup.

My father's cap was pushed to the back of his head so that his forehead shone in the dim light, and he grinned over his cigarette at me with the serious preoccupation of a child who has no intention of obeying anyone. And why should he, I thought as I sat down just behind him and loosened the stopper on the Thermos. The five or six players still at the table casually appraised my presence to see if it had tipped the scales of their luck in an even more unfavorable direction. Then they tossed their cards aside, drew fresh cards, or folded.

In the center of the table were more blue chips, and poking out from my father's coat pocket I recognized the promissory slips he must have redeemed, for he leaned to me and in a low voice, without taking his eyes from his cards, said, "I'm having a hell of a good time. The time of my life."

He was winning. His face seemed ravaged by the effort, but he was clearly playing on a level that had carried the game far beyond the realm of mere card playing and everyone seemed to know it. The dealer cocked an eyebrow as I poured broth into the plastic Thermos cup and handed it to my father, who slurped from it noisily, then set it down.

"Tell the old kettle she's got to put up with me a few more years," he said, and lit up a fresh cigarette. His eyes as he looked at me, however, seemed over-brilliant, as if doubt, despite all his efforts, had gained a permanent seat at his table. I squeezed his shoulder and kissed him hurriedly on his forehead. The men kept their eyes down, and as I paused at the door, there was a shifting of chairs and a clearing of throats. Just outside the room I nearly collided with the barman, who was carrying in a fresh round of beer. His heavy jowls waggled as he recovered himself and looked hard at me over the icy bottles. Then he disappeared into the card room with his provisions.

I took the long way home, finding pleasure in the fact that at this hour all the stoplights had switched onto a flashing-yellow caution cycle. Even the teenagers who usually cruised the town had gone home or to more secluded spots. *Doubt*, I kept thinking as I drove with my father's face before me, that's the real thief. And I knew my mother had brought me home because of it, because she knew that once again a member of our family was about to be stolen.

Two more days and nights I ministered to my father at the card room. I would never stay long because I had the fear myself that I might spoil his luck. But many unspoken tendernesses passed between us in those brief appearances as he accepted the nourishment I offered, or when he looked up and handed me his beer bottle to take a swig from—a ritual we'd shared since my childhood.

My father continued to win—to the amazement of the local barflies who poked their faces in and out of the card room and gave the dwindling three or four stalwarts who remained at the table a commiserating shake of their heads. There had never been a winning streak like it in the history of the tavern, and indeed, we heard later that the man who owned the card room and tavern had to sell out and open a fruit stand on the edge of town as a result of my father's extraordinary good luck.

Twice during this period my mother urged the doctor to order my father home. She was sure my father would, at some fateful moment, risk the entire winnings in some mad rush toward oblivion. But his doctor spoke of a new "gaming therapy" for the terminally ill, based on my father's surge of energies in the pursuit of his gambling. Little did he know that my father was, by that stage, oblivious to even his winning, he had gone so far into exhaustion.

Luckily for my father, the hour came when, for lack of players, the game folded. Two old friends drove him home and helped him down from the pickup. They paused in the driveway, one on either side of him, letting him steady himself. When the card playing had ended there had been nothing for my father to do but to get drunk.

My mother and I watched from the window as the men steered my father toward the hydrangea bush at the side of the house, where he relieved himself with perfect precision on one mammoth blossom. Then they hoisted him up the stairs and into the entryway. My mother and I took over from there.

"Give 'em hell, boys," my father shouted after the men, concluding some conversation he was having with himself.

"You betcha," the driver called back, laughing. Then he climbed with his companion into the cab of his truck and roared away.

Tied around my father's waist was a cloth sack full of bills and coins which flapped and jingled against his knees as we bore his weight between us up the next flight of stairs and into the living room. There we deposited him on the couch, where he took up residence, refusing to sleep in his bed—for fear, my mother claimed, that death would know where to find him. But I preferred to think he enjoyed the rhythms of the household; from where he lay at the center of the house, he could overhear all conversations that took place and add his opinions when he felt like it.

My mother was so stricken by the signs of his further decline that she did everything he asked, instead of arguing with him or simply refusing. Instead of taking his winnings straight to the bank so as not to miss a day's interest, she washed an old goldfish bowl and dumped all the money into it, most of it in twenty-dollar bills. Then she placed it on the coffee table near his head so he could run his hand through it at will, or let his visitors do the same.

"Money feels good on your elbow," he would say to

them. "I played them under the table for that. Yes sir, take a feel of that!" Then he would lean back on his pillows and tell my mother to bring his guests a shot of whiskey. "Make sure she fills my glass up," he'd say to me so that my mother was certain to overhear. And my mother, who'd never allowed a bottle of whiskey to be brought into her house before now, would look at me as if the two of us were more than any woman should have to bear.

"If you'd only brought him home from that card room," she said again and again. "Maybe it wouldn't have come to this."

This included the fact that my father had radically altered his diet. He lived only on greens. If it was green he would eat it. By my mother's reckoning, the reason for his change of diet was that if he stopped eating what he usually ate, death would think it wasn't him and go look for somebody else.

Another request my father made was asking my mother to sweep the doorway after anyone came in or went out.

"To make sure death wasn't on their heels; to make sure death didn't slip in as they left." This was my mother's reasoning. But my father didn't give any reasons. Nor did he tell us finally why he wanted all the furniture moved out of the room except for the couch where he lay. And the money, they could take that away too.

But soon his strength began to ebb, and more and more family and friends crowded into the vacant room to pass the time with him, to laugh about stories remembered from his childhood or from his nights as a young man at the country dances when he and his older brother would work all day in the cotton fields, hop a freight train to town and dance all night. Then they would have to walk home, getting there just at daybreak in time to go straight to work again in the cotton fields.

"We were like bulls then," my father would say in a

burst of the old vigor, then close his eyes suddenly as if he hadn't said anything at all.

As long as he spoke to us, the inevitability of his condition seemed easier to bear. But when, at the last, he simply opened his mouth for food or stared silently toward the far wall, no one knew what to do with themselves.

My own part in that uncertain time came to me accidentally. I found myself in the yard sitting on a stone bench under a little cedar tree my father loved because he liked to sit there and stare at the ocean. The tree whispered, he said. He said it had a way of knowing what your troubles were. Suddenly a craving came over me. I wanted a cigarette, even though I don't smoke, hate smoking, in fact. I was sitting where my father had sat, and to smoke seemed a part of some rightness that had begun to work its way within me. I went into the house and bummed a pack of cigarettes from my brother. For the rest of the morning I sat under the cedar tree and smoked. My thoughts drifted with its shiftings and murmurings, and it struck me what a wonderful thing nature is because it knows the value of silence, the innuendos of silence and what they could mean for a word-bound creature such as I was.

I passed the rest of the day in a trance of silences, moving from place to place, revisiting the sites I knew my father loved—the "dragon tree," a hemlock which stood at the far end of the orchard, so named for how the wind tossed its triangular head; the rose arbor where he and my mother had courted; the little marina where I sat in his fishing boat and dutifully smoked the hated cigarettes, flinging them one by one into the brackish water.

I was waiting to know what to do for him, he who would soon be a piece of useless matter of no more consequence than the cigarette butts that floated and washed against the side of his boat. I could feel some action accumulating in me through the steadiness of water raising and lowering the boat, through the sad petal-fall of roses in the arbor and the tossing of the dragon tree.

That night when I walked from the house I was full of purpose. I headed toward the little cedar tree. Without stopping to question the necessity of what I was doing, I began to break off the boughs I could reach and to pile them on the ground.

"What are you doing?" my brother's children wanted to know, crowding around me as if I might be inventing some new game for them.

"What does it look like?" I said.

"Pulling limbs off the tree," the oldest said. Then they dashed away in a pack under the orchard trees, giggling and shrieking.

As I pulled the boughs from the trunk I felt a painful permission, as when two silences, tired of holding back, give over to each other some shared regret. I made my bed on the boughs and resolved to spend the night there in the yard, under the stars, with the hiss of the ocean in my ear, and the maimed cedar tree standing over me like a gift torn out of its wrappings.

My brothers, their wives and my sister had now begun their nightly vigil near my father, taking turns at staying awake. The windows were open for the breeze and I heard my mother trying to answer the question of why I was sleeping outside on the ground—"like a damned fool" I knew they wanted to add.

"She doesn't want to be here when death comes for him," my mother said, with an air of clairvoyance she had developed from a lifetime with my father. "They're too much alike," she said.

The ritual of night games played by the children went on and on long past their bedtimes. Inside the house, the kerosene lantern, saved from my father's childhood home, had been lit—another of his strange requests during the time before his silence. He liked the shadows it made and the sweet smell of the kerosene. I watched the darkness as the shapes of my brothers and sister passed near it, gigantic and misshapen where they bent or raised themselves or crossed the room.

Out on the water the wind had come up. In the orchard the children were spinning around in a circle, faster and faster until they were giddy and reeling with speed and darkness. Then they would stop, rest a moment, taking quick ecstatic breaths before plunging again into the opposite direction, swirling round and round in the circle until the excitement could rise no higher, their laughter and cries brimming over, then scattering as they flung one another by the arms or chased each other toward the house as if their lives depended on it.

I lay awake for a long while after their footsteps had died away and the car doors had slammed over the goodbyes of the children being taken home to bed and the last of the others had been bedded down in the house while the adults went on waiting.

It was important to be out there alone and close to the ground. The pungent smell of the cedar boughs was around me, rising up in the crisp night air toward the tree, whose turnings and swayings had altered, as they had to, in order to accompany the changes about to overtake my father and me. I thought of my great-grandfather bathing with his horse in the river, and of my father who had just passed through the longest period in his life without the clean feel of cards falling through his hands as he shuffled or dealt them. He was too weak now even to hold a cigarette; there was a burn mark on the hardwood floor where his last cigarette had fallen. His winnings were safely in the bank and the luck that was to have saved him had gone back to that place luck goes to when it is finished with us.

So this is what it comes to, I thought, and listened to

the wind as it mixed gradually with the memory of children's voices which still seemed to rise and fall in the orchard. There was a soft crooning of syllables that was satisfying to my ears, but ultimately useless and absurd. Then it came to me that I was the author of those unwieldy sounds, and that my lips had begun to work of themselves.

In a raw pulsing of language I could not account for, I lay awake through the long night and spoke to my father as one might speak to an ocean or the wind, letting him know by that threadbare accompaniment that the vastness he was about to enter had its rhythms in me also. And that he was not forsaken. And that I was letting him go. That so far I had denied the disreputable world of dancers and drunkards, gamblers and lovers of horses to which I most surely belonged. But from that night forward I vowed to be filled with the first unsavory desire that would have me. To plunge myself into the heart of my life and be ruthlessly lost forever.

King Death

It was five-thirty and the sun was just coming up when I heard Dan brace his ladder outside against the bedroom wall. His paint bucket clanged against the rungs. I'd been dreaming. Something about dressing myself, then finding later that I hadn't dressed myself. Nobody in the dream minded that I was half-dressed, but I minded. Leonard was on his side, with his hands up near his chest. He was grinding his teeth. I gave him a little nudge with my knee and he stopped.

I got up, put my robe on, and went to make the coffee. Dan passed the kitchen window on his way to get something from his truck. We waved good morning and smiled at each other. I liked having him around the house. He was a hard worker; he had just gotten married and was doing odd jobs in addition to his regular one with the city parks department.

I let Leonard sleep. I knew the light falling across the bed would wake him soon enough. I took a glass of juice out to Dan.

"Going to get hot," he said. "I should start at midnight and work till daylight."

"Then you'd have to fight the bugs," I said. "If it's not one thing, it's two dozen others."

"I don't mind bugs," he said. "You can kill a few bugs and feel better, but you can't kill sun. It's going to get hot as Hades pretty soon." Dan was a Mormon, so he was always careful about what he said. He used the words "darn" and "shucks" a lot.

Dan was helping me to get the house ready to sell. Leonard designed heating and air-conditioning systems for industrial buildings, and he was due to be transferred to Dallas in the next couple of months. The transfer meant a promotion for him, so he was glad about it. If every move we'd made had meant a promotion, Leonard would have been president of the company. But most of the time the bosses were just shifting personnel here and there to cover themselves.

I met Dan a year ago, when we first moved to Tucson. Leonard and I had closed on the house deal and then driven back to Sacramento to pack things up for the move. But before the movers could get our things to Tucson, the house was vandalized—the living room carpet slashed, light fixtures broken, cabinet doors yanked off, handprints smeared on the walls. The neighbors said it must have been the gang of young men who'd rented the house before we bought it. They'd had wild parties. Sometimes as many as fifty cars and motorcycles would be parked along the street.

"We weren't about to mess with them," the man across

the street told me. "We saw all kinds of things. Thugs like that run in a pack. They wouldn't think twice about cutting your throat. I got kids and a wife and a home to think about. No, they made their music day and night, and we put up with it."

Leonard wanted to sell the house immediately. He was spooked by the fact that it had been broken into. But I didn't want to be run out of a house before I'd even lived in it. I said I'd take charge of fixing the place up again. It was going to be a nice place, I told him. I got Dan's name from a man at the hardware store, and Dan came to paint the inside of the house. Leonard and I stayed in a motel for two weeks, eating restaurant food and watching TV in bed at night. It wasn't so bad. Now, a year later, Dan was painting the outside. The house was starting to look so good I wanted to forget about having to move again.

"You got yourself a new neighbor," Dan said to me. He was resting his glass on a rung of the ladder.

"What do you mean?" I asked.

"There's somebody in the alleyway between your house and the next one," Dan said. "I saw him from the ladder while I was painting."

There was a high board fence around the house. It was over my head and nearly over Dan's head, too. The property had been fenced to leave a wide fire lane between our house and the house of a neighbor who called himself the Mad Hatter. He was a middle-aged disc jockey. He probably had a real name, but on the radio he called himself the Mad Hatter and that's all we ever knew him by. His mailbox had recently been vandalized, and he told me he was going to shoot the next kids he caught messing with it. He didn't care if they were in diapers, he said; he was going to plug them.

Dan motioned toward the fence and shook his head. "He's just as comfortable as a king," he said. "He's laying over there sleeping on his back, this old guy."

"On the ground?" I said. "With no covers?"

"Just his clothes," Dan said. "It's nobody I know," he added, and laughed. He drank down the last of his juice.

"You hold the ladder," I said. I cinched my robe around my waist and went up the ladder just far enough to see over the fence. There in the tall grass was a man lying face up with his eyes closed. One big-knuckled hand was stretched out in the grass. The other lay across his chest. He was using a flattened-out cardboard box for a bed. Paper wrappers and some wine bottles lay near him. I looked down at Dan and lowered my voice. "Maybe he's dead," I said.

"No, he moved," Dan said. "I just saw him move."

"He could die over there and not be found for days," I said. "He's probably been smoking in that high grass." I remembered how when I was a child the railroad bums had come up to our back fence and my mother had gone into the house and gotten slices of bread for them. She was superstitious about beggars. She believed that if you turned them away they'd put a curse on you. But instead my father cursed at her, and said he didn't buy bread so she could hand it away to every down-and-outer who passed the fence.

I went inside and woke Leonard. It was time for him to get ready for work anyway. I followed him into the bathroom and talked to him while he splashed water on his face. "There's a bum sleeping on the other side of our fence," I said. "I want you to go out there before you leave for work and tell him he can't sleep there. He can't make a bedroom out of our yard."

"Maybe he's just passing through," Leonard said. "I need a clean towel." He turned to me with his eyes squinted shut and water dripping onto his chest.

I handed him a towel from the cupboard near the medicine cabinet. "He'll tell his bum pals about this place," I said. "I don't want him out there. We'll never sell the house. Can you imagine me showing people around and saying, 'Oh and the fellow right here over the fence— that's our resident bum'?"

"I'll take care of it," Leonard said.

I went back into the kitchen to fix some eggs and toast. Leonard came in, smelling of shaving lotion. "Some neighborhood we landed in," he said. He pulled out his chair and sat down at the table. "We should never have moved into this house. You'll listen to me now."

"It's like this all over," I said. "Jeana, right next to the university, she told me that little nurse next door to her woke up with a man standing over her bed. It was the middle of the night. The nurse asked him what he wanted. She stayed calm the whole time. He said he was looking for his friend John. 'John doesn't live here,' the nurse told him. 'I think you better leave,' she said. So the man left, all right—with her stereo, her hair dryer, some eggs, and a pair of fingernail clippers. She was lucky she wasn't killed. He'd cut a hole in a screen on one of the living room windows and crawled in."

"We may as well live in Alaska," Leonard said. "It's worse than Alaska. It's lawless here. It's like the Old West. Like the Gold Rush all over again. Two thousand people a month moving into this place. It's a wonder they don't put tents on our lawn."

"Some of them don't even have tents," I said. I pointed my spatula toward the alley.

"I know, I know. I'll take care of it," he said.

In a little while he picked his car keys off the counter, gave me a kiss on the cheek, and headed outside. I went into the bedroom and opened the blinds. Leonard was at the fence. He'd taken a cigarette out and was lighting it. Then a head came up on the other side of the fence.

The bum had short white hair, and his face was tanned and wrinkled. I could see a white stubble of beard. The bum was squinting at Leonard. Then one of his hands came up over the fence and he took a cigarette from the pack Leonard held out to him. Leonard steadied the bum's hand until he could get the cigarette lit. The window was up, so I could hear through the screen some of what they were saying. Something about the V.A. hospital. The bum was saying he was going to have to go there. Leonard was smoking and listening. Then he nodded and said yes, he knew what it was to be hooked on booze.

"I was a practicing alcoholic for fifteen years," I heard my husband say. It was a history he gave every now and then—mostly when he heard somebody was having trouble with drinking. It made me mad sometimes to hear him say he was an alcoholic, as if it were a kind of reverse status. But I knew it was serious business—that he'd got out of the drinking and managed to stay out. His recovery happened a few years before we met, and this made it hard for me to appreciate how much he'd changed. I believed it, but only because he told me he'd been another person then. If he hadn't kept telling me about it—what an awful drunk he used to be—I would have forgotten. I guess that's what I wanted.

"I'd do anything for a drink," the bum said. "Oh, it's the Devil's juice, don't I know it. But I tell you, I'd kill for a drink. There's times I want it that bad," he said.

"Well, you get yourself in there to the hospital and let them help you," Leonard said. Then he took some money out of his billfold and gave it to the bum, along with the pack of cigarettes.

"What's your name?" the bum asked.

"Leonard."

"Put her there, Leonard," he said. Leonard took his hand. "I won't forget this," the bum said. "I used to be somebody myself once," he said. "I might pull out of this yet. You know what it is, don't you, to be drowned alive like this? I can tell you do. It's in your eyes. You know about it. I thank you," he said. "I thank you."

◆-◆-◆

About noon Dan came into the house. He'd been paint-ing the trim on the shady side of the house.

"Is he gone?" I asked.

"Yes," Dan said. "He went off toward the boulevard. But he'll be back."

"How do you know?" I said.

"If you give them money they always come back," he said. "Give them anything but money." He went over to the sink and drew himself a glass of water. When he got ready to go back to work I walked outside with him and went over to the fence. I lined up my eye with a knothole. In the fire lane I could see the flattened cardboard box. The grass was crushed down, and I counted four empty wine bottles.

"You know that doughnut stand over by the park?" Dan asked. "Well, it's open twenty-four hours. That's where these transients—we call them blanket people—that's where they go to stay warm in the winter. They must be feeding them doughnut holes over there," he said. He laughed, and pulled the bill of his blue work cap.

When Leonard came home from work, I asked him what the bum had said.

"I told him he'd have to move on," Leonard said. "I told him he should get some help for his drinking. He said he was a vet, was in Korea. He's only fifty-five, but he looks like King Death himself. I'd say seventy if I had to guess."

"Did he say anything else?" I asked. I was at the kitchen table shelling fresh peas into an aluminum bowl.

"Just that he used to have a house, kids, a wife—the whole works."

"I heard him say he'd kill for a drink," I said. I tossed an empty pod onto a newspaper on the floor.

"That was a figure of speech," Leonard said. "I don't

think he'd hurt anybody. He just wants enough to drink, and maybe some cigarettes."

"Dan says he'll be back. He says if you give them money they come back."

"I could be where he is, but for the grace of God," Leonard said.

"You were never that bad," I said.

"In a way, I was worse," he said. "I blamed it all on somebody else. I made somebody who loved me pay and pay hard."

"I'm glad I didn't know you then," I said.

"I'm glad, too," he said.

I bundled up the empty pods in the newspaper and stuffed them into a garbage bag near the back door. I was thinking that I wouldn't have stuck it with Leonard in those days. I would have let him down and I was ashamed, knowing that. But it was true.

I was drying my hands on the towel near the sink. Leonard came over to me at the sink and turned me toward him. He put his arms around me and held me in close under his chin. I kept my eyes closed. We stood still and hugged each other.

One morning we'd just finished breakfast and Leonard was on the phone talking long-distance when someone knocked on the door. I pulled the curtain back and saw the bum. He hadn't been around for at least a week. I'd kept checking the fire lane to make sure. I opened the door a crack.

"Is Leonard here?" the bum asked. His eyes were the bluest blue I'd ever seen—two caves of blue. I shut the door and went into the kitchen.

"Leonard," I said. "It's him. King Death."

Leonard put his hand on the receiver. "Tell him just a minute," he said.

I went back to the door and opened it. "Just a minute,"

I said. Then I shut the door and sat down near the window, where I could see him standing on the porch. He looked like one of those dogs you see tied to parking meters, waiting for somebody to come back.

Leonard came out of the kitchen. He opened the door and stepped onto the porch. "Here," Leonard said. He handed the bum some money. "Take this and don't come back," he said.

"You're God's own," the bum said.

"Don't come back, now," Leonard said. "You understand me?"

"I got you, friend. Don't you worry," the bum said. I stood up, so I could see through the open door. The bum was walking backwards toward the street. "You touched my heart," he called out to Leonard. "Yes, you did."

Leonard came back inside. He shook his head and reached for a cigarette from a pack on the counter. "It's like being hunted," he said. "He's like a piece of the past that nearly happened. It hunts you down and tries to move in."

"Don't give him any more money," I said. "I like your goodness. I admire it. But you can't really do anything for him. Not in the long run."

"No, nothing that lasts," Leonard said. "He'll cash it in out there. He'll just lie down with his bottle, and some morning he won't wake up."

Leonard's company needed him a month early, so the transfer went through before I'd sold the house. Leonard drove to Dallas and I stayed behind to supervise the last of the repairs. Dan was doing the work. With Leonard gone, it was good to have him around. I told him he should bring his new wife over for me to meet, and he joked with me, saying he didn't want to do that. She'd be too jealous. He'd never get in a day's work for me again.

One day I asked Dan to help me pick up all the papers and bottles in the fire lane. It was a mess.

"Shameful for any human being to live like this," Dan said. "You'd think salvation cost a million dollars, when it's free." That was the one thing about Dan that made me uncomfortable—how absolutely convinced he was about his salvation and about salvation being within everybody's reach. I'd given up talking to him about anything resembling religious matters. But once in a while I couldn't resist saying what I thought.

"It's a shame, all right," I said. "But maybe he's got to pay for his salvation in ways we can't even imagine. Or maybe he asked to be quits with drink but God turned him down."

"God's not like that," Dan said. "Ask, and ye shall receive."

"But he doesn't say *what* ye shall receive," I said. I'd carried a rake along and I was using it to scrape some broken glass into a little pile. I noticed how even the smallest pieces of glass glittered in the bright sunlight. "You might have to earn your salvation," I said. "You might have to go through some things before God would even turn his face in your direction."

"If he can save little children, he can save anybody anytime," Dan said. He was pulling a large cardboard box full of trash along the fence. He stopped and folded up the bum's cardboard bed and stuffed it into the box. Then he climbed into the box and jumped. He raised each foot up and brought it down hard.

"I don't believe salvation is something you get once when you're a kid, like the chicken pox, and then you're bound for Heaven," I said. "There are times you fail. Times nobody may know about. You've got to set yourself straight again and again." I looked up and saw that the Mad Hatter had come out of his house and was pacing along a row of pineapple palms he'd planted to let us know where his property line was. He walked over to the fire lane and stood with his hands on his hips, looking at the trash we were piling up.

"I'm going to get this grass mowed," I told him.

"Those hoodlum kids use this fire lane as a footpath," he said. "I've warned them. I told them I'll pull the trigger on them without batting an eye if they so much as set their big toe on my property." His face was puffy and he didn't stand still when he talked; he moved sideways, as if he were working up to something.

"You can't shoot to maim anymore," the Mad Hatter said. "You got to shoot to kill. Then you're O.K. If you just maim, they'll sue you for everything you've got. You have to kill them outright to stay within the law." Then he recited the findings of some court case he'd read about in the newspaper. Somebody who'd shot a robber in the arm and had to pay the hospital bill.

I never said anything when I heard him go into his tirades. I just nodded and got away from him as fast as I could. His wife locked him out of the house sometimes. I'd been woken up more than once when he was drunk and pounding on his own door to get in. One time I heard glass breaking over there.

Dan and I carried the trash to the front of the lot. The Mad Hatter was striding along the fire lane with his eyes on the ground. I watched him cross onto his property and make the rounds of his palms, checking with the toe of his shoe to see if they were still tamped into the ground firmly.

I felt better once the fire lane had been cleared. Dan had a friend with a big mower, and I hired him to cut the grass. Then I had Dan stretch a length of barbed-wire fencing along the back of the property. Several people came to look at the house, and one young couple seemed particularly interested. Leonard and I talked on the phone, making plans for me to pack and call the movers as soon as the house was sold. I began sorting clothes, getting rid of a lot of winter things we'd kept in case we should ever get sent back to upstate New York. I packed the clothes in paper sacks—Leonard's wool trousers, neck scarves, several hand-knitted vests, odds and ends of things—and I was planning to take them to Goodwill.

Dan had just one more job to do on the house. He was going to repair some bathroom tiles. I was making jam on the morning he was supposed to come, when I heard a knock at the front door. I turned the burner off and went into the front room. I opened the door and there he was —King Death himself. But he was clean-shaven now, and he had on a white shirt with a spangled vest over it. He looked like a rich gypsy. His eyes hadn't changed, though. They were the only young thing about him. They sizzled with energy. I took a step back and pulled the door closed to a narrow opening for my eyes and mouth.

"Your husband, Leonard," he said. "Is he here?"

Before I could think, I'd said it—that Leonard didn't live here anymore. "He's moved away," I said. "He won't be back."

The man looked down at his feet as though he were embarrassed. I was panicky, thinking now he'd know that I was alone. I tried to figure how to put Leonard back in the picture.

"Tell him for me—tell Leonard when you see him— that I didn't want anything," he said. "Tell him I just stopped by to see him."

"Just a minute," I said. I closed the door and locked it. Then I went into the bedroom and got one of the sacks of clothes. There were some of my things in it and some of Leonard's, but I didn't take time to sort anything. I went back to the door, unlocked it, and pushed the sack through until I felt the man take it. "You might get some use out of these," I said. I was afraid and glad at the same time, but I was trying to keep from showing how I felt.

The man made a little bow with the sack in one arm. His eyes snapped down. "Thank you, ma'am. I thank you."

Then he turned and started down the walk. I watched him pass along the street a little way, then I shut the door and went to heat the jam again. I sat down at the kitchen table. The house seemed very quiet. Soon there was the soft burbling of the jam beginning to boil, but that was all. I thought of the man going somewhere behind a building or into the park and taking our clothes out of the sack, holding them up to himself, trying them on but having no mirror to look into. If Leonard had been there, I'd never have given the man anything.

The young couple finally decided to buy the house. The man was about twenty-five. He climbed onto the roof and said he thought the house should have a new roof. I said if he wanted a new roof he could put it on himself. "This house is for sale *as is*," I said. When he saw he couldn't bully me, he went ahead and offered what we were asking.

I'd backed the car to the end of the driveway and was about to head for the real-estate office to sign the papers when I spotted the bum again. He was knocking at the Mad Hatter's door, gazing across to our oleander bushes while he waited. He had on Leonard's wool slacks. It was ninety-degree weather. The slacks were drawn up around his waist with a length of white cord. He was wearing my black knit vest over Leonard's blue shirt.

I scooted over to the passenger side and rolled the window down. I sat there a minute waiting to see if anyone would answer the Mad Hatter's door. I hoped no one was home. I could hear the dogs barking inside the house, and then the door opened and the Mad Hatter appeared. "You want to get shot?" he said. "You know where you're standing?"

"I need a little help," the bum said.

"Just a minute," the Mad Hatter said. He shut the door. I heard the dogs start up again.

The bum looked up at the sky. Then he clasped his hands behind his back and waited. His having our clothes on made him seem somehow familiar, as if I ought to know his name and be able to call out to him. I thought of Leonard, the Leonard I had never known.

The Mad Hatter opened the door again. "You see this?" he said. "This is a Smith and Wesson .38. It's loaded. I'm going to count to ten and on the count of ten I'm going to fire it directly at you."

The bum did not move. He did not say anything, either. I couldn't see his face, but I could see the Mad Hatter's mouth counting. I got out of the car when he reached six. I walked into my driveway on seven and eight. I could see both their faces then. I knew there wasn't time to make it to the phone. I kept remembering what the Mad Hatter had said earlier about not maiming but shooting to kill. I could see the gun pointing at the bum's chest. He was looking straight at the Mad Hatter. The Mad Hatter had said *nine* some time ago.

"Ten," said King Death.

Then he held there a minute, looking past the Mad Hatter. It was as if he were looking right through the house and out the back. Finally, he turned and began to walk toward the street. The Mad Hatter stood in the doorway holding the gun. He took a step forward onto the porch. The gun was aimed at the man's back. I thought of the bullet going through my vest and through Leonard's blue shirt, knocking the man down. Then the Mad Hatter turned and the gun began to drift slowly toward me. I stood still. I could feel my strength slipping from me. It was as though I were there and not there at the same time. The gun was trained on me. I had nothing, was nothing. I wanted to call out, "It's me! It's me, your neighbor." But I couldn't make any words. The Mad Hatter raised the gun over his head. A bullet cracked out of it. I looked up into the sky where the bullet must have gone. There were no clouds. There was nothing to see.

"It's loaded!" he called. "You better believe it's loaded. All of you!"

I was still looking up at the sky. I heard the door close and it was quiet a minute. Then I heard the yipping and whining of the dogs.

I stood a moment in the driveway, trying to think what to do with myself. I saw my car sitting near the street, where I'd left it. I made my way slowly toward it. I got inside and sat behind the wheel. The seat was hot. I closed my eyes. I put my hands on the wheel and turned it as I sat there. I felt like I'd died and come to life in the front seat of a car in a strange city. I opened my eyes and looked up at my house. It seemed far away and nowhere I'd ever lived.

Recourse

Jewel Kirk, my neighbor, was sleeping nights on my couch while she tried to find a buyer for her tavern. I was having my own sale—a garage sale. Word had spread and there were only a few odds and ends left, most of it from my married life with Velda. Velda had been dead six years so this was something I'd needed to do for a long time. It was hard, but it had to be done. Jewel had been my employer. I'd worked for her while she was running the tavern. But events during the past weeks had changed our lives considerably.

Three years before, Jewel had moved into her father's place next door—she and her husband, Burt. It was a surprise to both Jewel and me to find ourselves neighbors after forty-five years. When we were kids we never guessed we'd grow up, go away, and eventually come back to live alongside each other on the Little Niangua River. Anyway, there we were, farmland on either side of us and the nearest house a half mile away.

Now, three years later, Jewel was sleeping nights on my couch, and we were going to do something even farther from anything we'd imagined. When all our affairs were settled, we were going to California! Jewel had already settled more things than anyone in the county had been ready to witness. I'd overheard a number of views on her recent actions down at the coffee shop. The coffee drinkers were taking sides on what Jewel had done to her wayward husband, Burt. They'd shake their heads and take a sip of their coffee. "She's a chip off the old block, that Jewel," they'd say. The "old block" they were talking about was Jewel's father, Ed Kirk. He had the distinction of being remembered as the meanest man in Dallas County. The theory down at the coffee shop was that this explained a lot about Jewel Kirk.

But I had another view of Jewel, though I kept it to myself. What was the point of trying to tell these coffee drinkers anything when they'd already made up their minds about it? Jewel was somebody I trusted and understood to a good degree, even when she went out of bounds, which had happened fairly often of late. On the other hand, Burt and I had drawn the line almost from the minute we laid eyes on each other.

We'd first met up near the trash barrels out back after he and Jewel moved into the house next door. I noticed he was wearing gloves. Not workman's gloves, but leather gloves with little machine-made holes in them—driving gloves, he called them. This was enough for me, those gloves, and the way he went around day in and day out in a flat cap like you see Frenchmen wearing in the movies. He didn't improve on things when he opened his mouth, either. Once he'd come over and complained to me about my dandelions. I had a few that I regularly missed when I mowed because the lawn rose sharply around back of the house where it bordered on a field, and it was hard to lift the mower up there. Besides, dandelions are pretty. Next to the fields and pastureland they didn't look out of place. I'd just finished mowing one day when Burt knocked on my door.

"Those dandelions are blowing onto my lawn," he said. "I'm getting dandelions at the side of my house." I knew it was Jewel's lawn and Jewel's house so what he said hit me wrong. So did the fact that Burt never did anything around there but mow the damn lawn and empty the trash in his leather gloves. His driving gloves—which was pretty funny since neither he nor Jewel owned a car. I told Burt those dandelions must have blown in from the Davidsons' field since I always mowed everything down to the nub. He just shook his head, and turned and walked back the way he'd come.

All in all I felt I'd made a good decision when I'd sold the place Velda and I had in Lebanon and bought this house next to the old Kirk place in the area where I'd grown up. I had lots of memories about this land along the Little Niangua River. Things like fording the river on my horse to visit Jewel and her sisters. (I was especially interested in the sister nicknamed Pebble.) I also prowled the Indian caves around here, hunting for arrowheads. Things like that. My own father had shoed horses. He'd gotten along with everybody, even Jewel's father. I used to go with him to steady the horses while he worked.

"There's a curse on that family," my father would say after we'd leave from doing a day's work for Ed Kirk. He was referring to the fact that all the Kirk children, excepting Jewel, had this bone disease that caused their joints to freeze up. There were six girls, counting Jewel, and one boy, Grover. The girls, all of them except Pebble, had been lucky enough to find someone. After they got married, they all lived in and around Dallas County. Pebble was different in every way, and she'd managed to make it on her own. She worked as a teller in a bank and learned to save her money. That's how she eventually moved to California. Grover had died when he was twenty, and the girls, who were women now, still suffered various degrees of disability as a result of the bone disease. Two of them were in wheelchairs and one had been in Kansas City for some time in a hospital. In the days when we'd been children, Jewel's father had rounded the kids up and loaded them into the wagon. He'd driven them fifty miles to Kansas City to a clinic. I remember they stopped at our house to get my dad to mend the harness before they started out. "He must have cared about those kids," my father said afterwards.

When a story was told by one of the neighbors about terrible Ed Kirk, my father would remind the person of that trip to the clinic with a wagonload of crippled children. But it was the only evidence I ever heard offered in Ed Kirk's defense. He quarreled with neighbors on all sides of him. He'd been known to kill the prize cow of one of his neighbors. Once he'd even dammed the Little Niangua River with staves until it flooded another neighbor's barnyard. But these were small offenses compared to the time he outright shot a man in town after the man made an indecent overture to one of his daughters, then turned around the next minute and called her a hopeless cripple. The insult to his daughter had happened several years before, but Ed Kirk hadn't forgotten. He met the man in an alleyway and shot him without so much as a how-do-you-do. There'd been a trial in Bolivar over in the next county. But the dead man had been carrying a gun, and since nobody had actually witnessed the shooting, Ed Kirk went free.

Pebble was Jewel's youngest sister. I always had an eye

out for her in those days. I guess that's what made those trips to the Kirk place so memorable. Pebble would drag and hop her way out from the house to bring my father and me lunch while my father was there shoeing horses. She'd sit with us under a big walnut tree while we ate. She had nice features and a sweet disposition. Her arms and legs were contorted but, for all that, she seemed to manage okay.

"She's like this tree I saw once," my father said. "It's when I was back East that time, and they took me to the ocean. There was this tree on a bluff. The wind shaped that tree. You looked at it and you knew something. You knew that tree didn't have a choice in the way it grew. If I ever get back East again, I'd like to go take another look at that tree."

After Pebble had saved enough money to make her move to California, Jewel used to send me news about her. She knew Pebble and I'd been sweet on each other. This was after I was married and had my own life. Velda and I were living in Lebanon then. But Jewel was a great one to keep in touch. Every year she'd send a card on my birthday, in addition to her other cards and letters. She wrote me that Pebble lived in Huntington Beach, California, and that she worked assembling electronic parts of some sort. People she worked with picked her up and drove her to the job and afterwards drove her home again. Then, my wife and I went to Leadmine for Decoration Day services. These services were held at the church I'd gone to as a kid. I saw Jewel during the course of the activities. She told me that Pebble had been banished from the family by their father. Before the old man died, he struck out at everybody who'd given help to his wife after the two of them split up. Pebble was living in California at the time, had been for twenty years. She paid her mother's way to California and nursed her right to the end. The mother was a great hulk of a woman and I often wondered how Pebble, a small thing and with that bone disease, ever managed to take care of the old woman. It would have made more sense for Jewel to have taken it on. Jewel was a big woman. But Jewel was her father's favorite because, some said, she was the only one of the children who wasn't cursed with the bone disease.

Pebble was nobody's favorite but mine. I'd tried to court her, in my own way, back there in my teens. "Oh Johnny," she'd say to me when I brought her some toilet water, or a bunch of daisies, the least little thing. "You shouldn't have done it," she'd say. She had big green eyes. Her eyes were the color of a pond where I used to take her catfishing. "I love your eyes," I told her one day, before I could stop myself. She just smiled, like she knew everything good and bad in the world and then some.

"You mean my bullfrog eyes?" she said, and laughed. I threw a rock into the pond and tried to pretend I hadn't said anything.

Pebble's father caught on to me, the way I kept finding excuses to come around for first one thing, then another. The last time I was allowed on the place I'd come over with a baby squirrel some dogs had mauled. It was just the sort of creature Pebble loved to fuss over.

"What you got in that cage?" he asked me.

"A baby squirrel, for Pebble," I said.

"Well, you can turn right around with it," he said. He shot a stream of tobacco into the bushes next to the porch. He stood there on the porch glaring at me. "Pebble's got work to do. You keep to home from now on," he said.

I took the long way home that day, following the river, carrying the squirrel. About halfway home I just couldn't bear the cries of the thing and I turned it loose. It half rolled, half scuttled into the bushes.

After Velda died, and Jewel came to live in her family's home next door, we used to sit out on the porch of her house. Burt would be inside watching television. "I don't know how we lived through it," Jewel would say, talking about her childhood. Then she'd tell stories about her father making her and Pebble and the rest of them carry staves on their backs to build fences. "And remember," she'd say, "these children were crippled." I reminded Jewel of how she'd bring notes on horseback from Pebble to me. When I got married, Velda made me get rid of all those scraps of paper with Pebble's wobbly writing on them. Pebble never said much in the notes, just a few sentences. But she drew plenty of flowers and hearts at the bottom of the page and put her own two eyes into the drawings, like she was watching me as I read. There was a connection between us, Pebble and me, that seemed to survive in spite of the fact that we seldom saw each other. It was like that right up until the time Pebble left for California, and I met Velda, in that order. After that, Jewel more or less took over giving me the news on Pebble. I still felt affection for Pebble, but she was like somebody I wished well, but couldn't do anything for. How could I? I was a married man. Anyway, she seemed to be doing fine on her own.

At the time Jewel moved in next door with Burt, I was at loose ends. When I'd relocated back alongside the Little Niangua I'd brought a lot of Velda's things with me. I'd boxed them and stored them in the garage at the side of the house. I couldn't think what else to do with them. I had to climb over those boxes to plug in my power tools. When Velda was alive, I was always cursing these boxes of junk. But the thing that hit me after she died was how much pleasure she'd had from going to rummage sales, collecting everything from broken-down treadle sewing machines to fifteen yards of clothesline I'd never gotten around to stringing up. It was, I saw then, maybe her greatest pleasure. I gave a few items to Jewel, but the rest just stayed in the garage.

"You got to get busy," Jewel said to me one day when

we met at the side of the road near the mailboxes. I noticed her hair had only a little black left in the white, and it hit me that we were old, both of us. I remembered her long black pigtails. But they'd been cut ages ago, and those little flecks of black were all that was left of them. "You come down and help me at the tavern," Jewel said. "I'll put you to work."

I said, "I'll think about it."

I suppose people wondered why Jewel didn't put her husband to work. But he never showed his face at the tavern, and Jewel insisted that it be that way. She'd had one alcoholic husband, she said, and she didn't want another. Her first husband had fallen by the wayside early on, up in Kansas. Jewel had packed her bag and skipped out, the story went.

I thought it over and then told Jewel I'd work for her. The routine went like this. I'd get up at 5 A.M. and go with her to clean up at the tavern from the night before. There was a little grocery store addition at one side of the tavern that had to be opened for business at 8 A.M. Jewel kicked everybody out of the tavern at closing time and then went home herself. But the place was always in a hell of a shape when we got there the next morning. I'd open the door and walk into the stale beer and cigarette smell like somebody coming out onto a battlefield at dawn. There was everything in there but dead bodies. Sometimes I'd find items of clothing that made me think people had used the place for a dressing room. Those mornings it would occur to me to wonder about Burt, what he was doing while Jewel and I slaved away at the tavern and the store. He looked able enough to do clean-up work. But it was none of my business.

"He looks for work," Jewel would say, "but he can't find anything. He drives as far away as Liberty looking for work, but so far nothing." When she talked like that I knew she was worried, in spite of the face she put on things. I tried to do as much as I could to help her with the tavern, because there wasn't a thing I could do about Burt.

When he had worked, Burt had driven heavy equipment, cats and shovels, graders—that sort of thing. He didn't want to have to do anything else, Jewel said. She said she could understand that. She loved running her tavern and grocery, and she wouldn't like to have to stop and become, say, a beautician or a telephone operator—especially at her age. She thought Burt would get something, what he wanted, eventually.

But during this ''eventually,'' a lot of things were going on behind her back. A friend of mine in a town twenty miles away told me he'd seen my neighbor drinking in a bar there. At first I thought he meant Jewel. She'd been known to take a drink or two in other establishments, though she never drank in her own. But the neighbor in question was Burt. My friend said Burt had been in the company of a woman, and the description of the woman bore no resemblance to Jewel.

I began to feel even more uneasy about Jewel's married life when I looked over at her house in the middle of the day once, while Jewel was working, and saw a woman waiting in a car. The woman honked the horn. That's how I happened to look out. Burt came hopping down the steps, all spruced up, slid into the driver's seat and drove off with her. I was working that night with Jewel at the tavern, so I don't know how or when or even *if* Burt got back. I do know there were no lights in their house when I drove into my driveway and Jewel got out and walked next door. Of course I didn't mention what I'd seen to Jewel. She'd find out soon enough.

The next day Jewel and I were carrying in some cases of beer from a delivery truck parked behind the tavern, and she said to me, out of the blue, ''Nobody ever wanted to go with me except some old drunk. And if they weren't a drunk to start with, they ended up that way." She was talking like she was closing a chapter on something she had to face up to. She was my friend and I was ready to listen. But that's all she said. She had a case of beer on her shoulder and I had one on mine too. We were walking with our free shoulders side by side.

"Jewel," I said, "you got your name for a reason. You're a jewel in my book." She gave me a stiff little grin, and I knew that too much had happened to her for that kind of remark to go far, but I think she appreciated it anyway. She just hoisted the beer onto the stack in the storage room and went to the truck for more.

It got to be general knowledge before long that Burt had a woman over in Jefferson County. He was drinking with her in public places. But his carousing time was seriously cut down when he finally got a job with the highway department. That must have made him careless or desperate, trying to find time to meet the woman and also hold down a job—not to mention the fact that he was married.

One night it was so slow at the tavern I said to Jewel, "Why don't you take the night off? I'll close up." So she went home and caught the two of them, her husband and his new woman, on the premises. When Jewel told me about it, she said she'd thrown a kettle of spaghetti over the two of them. It was cold spaghetti, she said, but it did her heart good anyway. Burt, knowing Jewel's temper, must have imagined she'd be standing by the front door with a butcher knife, because while he and his woman were cleaning spaghetti off themselves, Jewel could hear a squabble going on. Burt was telling the woman they'd have to climb out the bedroom window and the woman was saying it would ruin her dress. Jewel went around to the back next to the window. Pretty soon the woman was hanging from the windowsill with Jewel cussing and throwing things at her. Burt got his share too when he jumped down. Somehow the two of them made it away in the woman's car.

Two weeks after Burt cooked his goose with Jewel, nothing appeared to have changed over there—though it had. Burt was gone, but his heavy equipment was still sitting in front of the house. Jewel had called the highway department to get them to come and move it. The equipment belonged to them. But the machines were still sitting there looking like a couple of dinosaurs. Jewel would look at that equipment and make threats. Another week passed and the equipment still hadn't been moved.

It was about this time that Pebble came home from California. Jewel had told her about the entire mess, and Pebble had taken her vacation early and come out to give her sister some support. She still had those green bull-frog eyes, but of course she'd aged, like the rest of us. Her limbs were even more crooked than I'd remembered. Still, she had a good strong manner—something I'd loved about her from the beginning. We were glad to see each other. I squeezed her hand and she smiled at me in a way that made me remember those hearts and flowers at the bottom of her notes. But we didn't have much time to talk. I was doing the biggest share of work at the tavern while Jewel tried to get herself right side up. She'd hired a lawyer and was trying to undo a bad situation. And I don't just mean the marriage to Burt, though that was the heart of her trouble. It seems Jewel had signed over the house to Burt in order to avoid paying inheritance tax on the place. Since the marriage had gone to hell, Burt informed Jewel he intended to move into the house with his new sweetheart, once he got Jewel out. Legally, he said, it was his. It was an awful mess. Pebble was doing her best to calm Jewel down, but without much success. And who could blame Jewel? It wasn't the kind of thing you could take lying down. It hurt her self-respect, and it threatened to put her out on the street.

One night I was lying in bed when I heard an ungodly racket next door. It was nearly three o'clock. I knew the tavern was closed and that Jewel must be hearing the racket too. I looked out the window. I could see somebody holding a flashlight and somebody else up on one of those big graders. I could see the beam of light skipping around over the huge tires of the thing. Then I heard glass breaking and the sound of metal being hammered. Finally, I could make out that it was Jewel doing the hammering. She was up on the machine near the controls, pounding the living daylights out of it with a sledgehammer. The fury of that noise was awful. I was glad there was nobody else close enough to hear it. When Jewel finished with that machine, she went on to the other one, a big dozer with a shovel on the front. Whoever held the flashlight was nervous—the light was jumping all over the place. But every now and then I'd get a glimpse of Jewel's arm on the hammer. It came down again and again onto the machine. This time it was headlights I heard breaking. I walked onto my porch to get a better look, but then the flashlight went out. I stood there listening. I could hear Pebble's voice pleading with Jewel. The lights in Jewel's house were off and so were mine. I felt I'd seen enough, though there was lots more to hear. I went back in and got into bed. After a while, the hammering stopped and I fell asleep.

The next morning I was almost afraid to look out. But when I did, I had to marvel. The heavy equipment in Jewel's yard was pretty well beaten up. I went out into the yard to get a better look.

I saw a pickup truck pull into Jewel's drive. It had a highway department insignia on the door. Two men got out of the cab with clipboards and moved toward the remains of the equipment. They shook their heads as they circled the machines, from time to time making notations on their clipboards. One of the men saw me wrestling the water hose over to some flowers. He called and waved, then started to walk in my direction. I acted senile, like I couldn't make out what the guy wanted. I turned and headed into the house.

Around noon Pebble limped over and said she needed me to drive her somewhere.

"I can't tell you where," she said. "You won't do it if I tell you. You'll just have to go this one blind, Johnny." Her green eyes looked tired, but there was enough mischief in them to get me to agree. I said I was having my coffee first, so she came into the kitchen and sat down.

"Somebody went to work on that machinery," I said. I poured her a cup of coffee and set it in front of her. "I guess you must have heard it all," I said. I was playing dumb and Pebble knew it.

"I called the highway department and the sheriff," Pebble said. "I told them it was vandals. That it must have happened while we were at the tavern. Jewel was going to tell them she'd done it. She said she didn't give a tinker's damn. It's terrible how this divorce thing is working on her." Pebble brushed her face with one of her crippled arms. "I couldn't stop her last night, Johnny. She feels she's got no recourse." Pebble folded her crooked arms and stared into her coffee cup. I was starting to fall in love with her all over again, right there in my kitchen. We finished our coffee, and I locked the back door. We went out the front, and I locked that door too. "Vandals," I said to Pebble and winked. Pebble shook her head. She situated herself in the front seat. I made sure she was comfortable, then shut the car door, went around and got in under the wheel.

"Now where?" I said. Pebble had an address scribbled on a piece of paper. She read it to me. It was an address in town, over near the municipal swimming pool. We saw herds of kids carrying towels and swimming suits as we got into the neighborhood.

"That's the house," I said, and Pebble leaned across me to check it out. It was a little shoebox of a house. Probably built after the war, sometime in the late forties.

"Doesn't look like a honeymoon cottage," Pebble said. Then I understood where we were. I expected Burt to step onto the porch any minute with his new woman. We crept along in the car.

"Keep going," Pebble ordered. "Now, pull into that alley." We turned off the street and drove until we got within a house or two of Burt's new residence.

"This'll do," Pebble said. I left the engine running and took a glance around the alley. A lot of garbage cans and brambles. There were kids' toys scattered in some of the yards. We could see a clothesline in Burt's yard, and on it were some of Burt's clothes I'd seen hanging on the line out behind Jewel's house. But there was a short white nightie next to one of Burt's denim work shirts. It was not part of Burt's regular wardrobe. Pebble had spotted the nightie too, and down the line there were items of clothing that didn't bear speculating on.

"I'm glad Jewel can't see this," Pebble said. "She'd put a torch to that house before you could say Jack Robinson —whoever he was."

We sat there a while longer, watching a breeze ruffle the clothes on the line. The white nightie billowed and fluttered against Burt's shirt sleeve, then went slack. I was nervous and looking for something to do. I saw the ashtray was full of Jewel's cigarette butts. I unhooked the thing and dumped the mess out the window into the alley.

"Would you mind telling me what we're doing?" I said to Pebble as I worked the ashtray back under the dashboard.

"We're kidnapping a dog," Pebble said, as if it were the most normal thing in the world. I was sorry I'd asked. Pebble looked over at me and said, "It isn't what you think." She had on a green pullover that matched her eyes, and I felt that connection from our childhood at work again, as if we had an invisible hookup to each other's feelings. There wasn't time to discuss the situation. The back door to Burt's house opened and his new woman stepped onto the porch in a housedress with big daisies on it. Right at her heels we could see a white toy poodle. The woman came off the porch and disappeared behind a bed sheet in the middle of the clothesline. The poodle was nosing the ground, frantically circling the woman's legs where they came down behind the sheet. The legs walked along the sheet and then the woman's head appeared above the white nightie. We could see that she was blond and had tight little curls all around her face. The rest of the hair puffed out like she still had to deal with it—spray it or whatever. Then Burt's woman unpinned the nightie and a few of Burt's things, turned and went back into the house.

The poodle was still in the yard, so I had the feeling the woman would be making more trips to the clothesline. Without a word, Pebble climbed out of the car. "Pebble," I said in a low voice. I saw her carry herself a few feet in front of the car and stop. Then she bent and patted her hip. I saw the poodle prick up its ears. Then I heard Pebble make a noise with her lips. The dog ran right into Pebble's arms. When she straightened and hobbled back to the car, it looked like she was carrying a stuffed animal. She let the dog into the car. It started to yip and show its little teeth the minute it laid eyes on me. Then it set those teeth into my arm just below the elbow. "God," Pebble said. I shook at the thing until it had mostly shirt sleeve. The car was elbows and fur for a few minutes. Finally, Pebble got the dog off me and under control. It rooted itself into her lap and sat down facing me. Then Pebble went and kissed the dirty thing right on its nose. It kept up an intermittent *err*ing sound as we drove back to my house. "That's a good dog," Pebble said every so often and cradled the poodle in her bent arms.

At my place Pebble let herself out of the car and carried the dog inside. The yipping noise the dog kept up was nothing anybody'd ever want to live with.

"It can't stay here," I said. "I don't have any use for this breed of dog." I was holding my elbow and wondering how deep its teeth had gone. Pebble was still cradling the menace. I wanted to fling the poodle into the yard and take her in my own arms—but now one of my arms was disabled. I pulled my shirt sleeve past the teeth marks. Pebble gave a little cry when she saw the bite. She carried the poodle into my bedroom, put it in there and shut the door. The poodle didn't like this one bit and yipped away some more.

Pebble attended to me. Her hands seemed to know everything about gentleness. The bone disease had skipped right over those sweet hands. Just as she finished swabbing my arm with disinfectant I grabbed up one of those hands and gave it a kiss. Pebble acted like it wasn't anything out of the ordinary, as if it was something I'd always been in the habit of doing. She rolled my sleeve down and I let her button the cuff for me. But right then, with that crazy dog yipping and those wrecked machines over in Jewel's yard, I felt like picking up my life again. I mean having somebody to love and to be with. But I didn't want to say anything right then.

"Jewel was going to poison that poor pup," Pebble said. "She set the poison out on the kitchen table this morning. She meant to do it. She was serious. All because the dog belonged to that woman, and the woman loved it more than anything—more even than Burt," Pebble said and laughed. She put the stopper into the bottle of disinfectant. I rubbed my arm. The bite was stinging but some-how it wasn't entirely unpleasant. I thought I should be feeling something out of the ordinary to go along with what I was thinking.

That night I slept on the couch and let the dog have the bedroom. I hoped it liked table scraps because that's all there was for it to eat. I put together an odd assortment of baloney and string beans and sprinkled it with bacon drippings. It didn't look half bad. Then I stuck my arm into the bedroom, set the dish down and jerked the door shut. Jewel had closed the tavern down for a week, so I had no place I needed to be. "Renovation," she'd written on the sign, but she didn't mean the tavern. I settled my-self onto the couch, and the last thought I had was that maybe in the morning I'd scramble some eggs for the dog and myself.

When Pebble came over the next day, she was all dressed up. "She looks cute enough to take on a honey-moon," I thought, but I just said, "That dog is driving me nuts."

"Can you take us to the airport?" she said. For a crazy minute I thought she was asking me to run off with her. I passed my hand over where there used to be hair during the days I'd been a young buck hanging around her door. Then, without letting me answer, Pebble walked toward the bedroom. The dog started to yip, and I understood I'd slipped off the track a considerable way.

In the car the dog behaved itself. It sighed and laid its nose across Pebble's arm.

"It's not good, Johnny," Pebble said. "Jewel could lose everything. I'm afraid for her peace of mind, but what can I do? I've got to go back to my job."

"Don't worry," I said, and patted her arm. "I'll stick by her." Pebble turned her big green eyes on me. She seemed to be thinking about something. I felt that a lot of unsaid things were getting said.

At the airport I helped her arrange for the dog, then saw it caged and wheeled away. Good! I thought. Then we checked Pebble's luggage. I was glad to have a few minutes alone with her. She leaned on my arm as we walked slowly to the gate area. I had her traveling case in the other hand.

"You call me, Johnny, when you hear what's happening," Pebble said. "In about a week there'll be a hearing to decide who gets the house. That's going to be rough," Pebble said. She started to take her traveling case from me. Then I reached out for her. I held her stiff body with its damaged bones close to me. Then I let go. Pebble suddenly gave a quick jerk of her head and landed a kiss on the highest point she could reach on my neck. "Will you write me, Johnny, or else call?" she said.

"You can count on it, Pebble," I said. "I've got some things to talk over with you." She gave my hand a squeeze. She stood like that with my hand a few moments, looking worried. Then she smiled. I watched her turn and move toward the gate. She moved quickly for somebody with her physical troubles. The other passengers stood aside for her like she was some kind of dignitary. And maybe she was. I thought so anyway.

When I got home I went into the bedroom to see what effect the dog's night in there'd had. My windup alarm clock was on its side with the hands stopped. I stepped over a puddle and noticed another puddle under the bed. I patted the bed with both hands to make sure that was dry. It was. My socks were scattered on the floor, but other than that, unless the dog had fleas, the place was going to be habitable again. I considered the likelihood of fleas and thought of buying some spray and giving the room a good going over.

During the week that followed, I called Pebble once, and that was to tell her that Jewel's hearing was set for

11 A.M. Friday. She asked me some questions about Jewel's state of mind. Then she told me about sanding down a little chest of drawers she'd bought at a lawn sale. I could hear the dog yipping in the background.

"I hope that poodle's not going to be a permanent resident," I said. But I didn't have any way to tell her what I really intended. I said I'd call her and let her know when the legal ownership of the house had been decided. It didn't help that the judge for the case was a brother to the manager of the division Burt worked for at the highway department.

The morning of the hearing I drove Jewel into town and dropped her off at the courthouse. I told her I'd pick her up when she called. But she never called. About noon I saw her steam into the house and slam the door. Somebody had brought her home, and I could tell she was in no mood to see anyone. I guessed the outcome of the hearing and decided to wait awhile before going over to hear the whole story.

I sat at the kitchen table and folded and unfolded my hands. I got to thinking about Pebble and what a long detour it had been to find her again. She'd been on her own for so long it made me afraid she wouldn't have me. We were old now, and we each had our ways of doing things. Suddenly I heard glass breaking outside. I looked out the window in time to see a chair sticking through the glass at one of Jewel's side windows. Then I heard glass breaking around to the far side of her house. I saw Jewel come outside and head for her garage. She came back carrying two paint buckets. I had an idea what she intended to do. But it was her business. I let her alone to do it.

By the time I went over there, the damage had been done. Jewel was standing in the ruination of her house, the very place she'd grown up in. She was holding an empty paint can. She had paint all over herself and over the floors and walls. She stared at me like she wanted to paint me too. For a minute we just stood there looking at each other. Then she started to cry and wipe at her face, still holding the paint can.

"Let him have the damn house now," she said. "Let her have it too." She started to walk toward me like a blind person. I stepped up to her and put my arm around her shoulders. I shook the paint can out of her hand and then I walked her, like that, with my arm around her shoulders, over to my place. When we got inside I sat her down in the kitchen. I went to the cupboard and brought down some whiskey and two glasses. We sat there working on the bottle, talking over what to do next. All the anger had gone out of her, and she wanted me to understand she was sane again and able to go on now. But *on to where?* she wanted to know. I said Pebble seemed to like it fine in California. And then I proposed something.

"Why don't we go out to California?" I said. "We'll start a tavern there." Maybe I was a little drunk by then.

She shook her head. Then she said, "We'll see." She passed her hand over the top of the table in front of her, as if she were wiping at something. She looked at me. "Things are finally working out for you and Pebble? I'm glad, Johnny."

"Nothing's been said one way or the other," I said. "No promises or questions yet. Just hopes."

Jewel held her whiskey up and gave it a little nod, a kind of toast, before she drank it. I remembered then what she'd said that morning earlier in the summer—how nobody could love her but old drunks. I knew Jewel deserved better than she was ever going to get. I noticed she was still flecked with paint. Also, there was a long white streak down the underside of one arm. I got up and found some turpentine under the sink. I handed it to her along with an old towel. She got up from the table and went into the bathroom to clean up. Meanwhile, I looked around in the cupboards for something to fix for supper. I took down two cans of chili, found a pan and the can opener and went to work. When the chili was hot, I put two bowls on the table and dished it up. Jewel still had paint in her hair and in the creases of her skin here and there, but she looked better. Her cheeks were pink where she'd rubbed to get the paint off.

After we'd eaten I left Jewel at the kitchen table. "Help yourself to that whiskey," I said. I went to the living room and made up a bed for her on the couch. Then I got ready for bed myself. In a few minutes I thought I heard Jewel open the front door and go out. I supposed she was stepping over to her house to get her night things.

I went out to the kitchen and drew a glass of water. It was then I glanced out the kitchen window to see if the lights were on over at Jewel's—but there was more than lights on. The entire back of the house was aflame. I could hear crackling and see angry spurts of fire darting through the windows. I dressed in a hurry and went out the back door. I started calling for Jewel. I was afraid she might not have been able to get herself out. Then I saw someone huddled where my dandelion patch is on the slope behind the house. The light from the flames brightened and flickered against the sky. It was Jewel all right. She was sitting with her arms around her legs, watching. I didn't say anything, just dropped down beside her and began to snap off the heads of a few dandelions. Jewel was rocking slightly, not taking her eyes off the burning house.

"I decided to finish it off," she said without looking at me. "I didn't do it mad, Johnny. I was right at the heart of calm when I did it."

I patted her on the knee, stood up, and offered my hand to her. She took it and raised herself up. By then there were neighbors driving down the road to park and watch. Someone had seen the flames and phoned the others. In the distance I could hear the yowling of fire engines as they turned off the main road and headed toward us. Jewel and I moved around to the front of my place and went inside. I gave her my jacket and she went out to stand near my car and watch the fire fighters go to work on saving what was left of her house. I couldn't think of it as Burt's house, no matter what the law had decided, and I guessed nobody else who knew the situation would either. The noise of water hoses spraying and men calling to each other kept up for hours. I stayed inside the house. After a long while Jewel came inside. We sat at the kitchen table with our coffee cups and watched until the last of the ladders had been taken away. There was nothing but the shell of a house with smoke leaking out of it here and there. Jewel was still wearing my jacket.

"I didn't know it would hurt so much, watching this," she said. "Daddy would have done the same thing though. There's nothing left now except California," she said. She roused herself and laughed.

I laughed too. Then I got up and rinsed out my coffee cup. A few birds were starting to chirp and a dawn half-light was coming into the window. I remembered I hadn't called Pebble. I wondered how she was going to take the news that the house was gone. I knew she was going to worry that Jewel would be arrested, but I was the only witness and I wasn't saying anything. Let them investigate till Hell freezes over, I thought.

"We'll call Pebble after we've had some sleep," I said. "We'll talk to her about California, and the possibilities for us out there." I found an old flannel shirt in the closet and a pair of my own pajama bottoms for Jewel. I didn't wait to see her get into them, and went about putting on my pajamas in the bedroom. When I was ready to turn off the light I called, "Good night." After a minute she said, "Good night." But her voice was muffled, and I think she was crying.

I pulled the covers over me and lay there. After a while I thought I felt something biting me. Damn fleas, I thought. I lay there with my mind empty awhile. Then I thought of the river, of leaving it behind, and I felt something that had nothing to do with California or anywhere else I might ever be. I was getting close to sleep, but I seemed to be moving through images of my young days on the Little Niangua River, of Pebble as a girl and then of Pebble's father, and how, like Jewel, I was soon to have the final word.

Turpentine

I WAS IN THE BASEMENT IN MY RAIN BOOTS when Tom called down that there was someone to see me. I was sloshing around in water that had a pink tinge to it. It didn't take a plumber to know it was lint from some red bath mats that had plugged the drain.

By the time I opened the door to the kitchen, Tom had gone back upstairs to his study. From where I stood, I could look through the kitchen and see a young woman sitting on the couch. She was staring at something out the window. She stood up when she saw me. While we were shaking hands she looked at my rain boots. I looked too. They were causing a puddle on the hardwood floor. I knew the kitchen tiles would be glistening with welts of water where I'd passed.

"A little crisis of the lower regions," I said. She squeezed my hand lightly, then took her hand back. It left a waxy feeling. "I'm Ginny Skoyles," I said.

"I'm your Avon Lady," the woman said. She was smiling now. I could see why Tom had let her in, even though he didn't like door-to-door people.

"So you really exist," I said. "I thought they'd just made you up, like Mister Clean. Do you have a name of your own?"

"Mary," she said. "Mary Leinhart."

She turned and moved back toward the couch, then sat down on the edge of the cushion. I pulled off my boots. I looked at her more closely then. She had large dark eyes and her skin was so white it was almost translucent. I thought of the word "alabaster."

"I live in the neighborhood," she said, "so I thought I'd stop in and show you a few things." She had a camel-colored sample case. She opened it across her lap and took out two catalogues. She was wearing a powder-blue nylon parka. It had zippers every which way on it, and I wondered what she might be keeping inside the pockets. She had on beige slacks and blue-striped sneakers.

"Maybe you'd like to look through these," she said. "There are some good sale items in soaps and talcs."

I looked at the top catalogue. The cover showed a red-nailed hand reaching out of the sky to set a box of talcum powder onto a crimson expanse of water. In the background were violet-blue mountains. The sky behind the mountains had the same tortured look as the water. The hand was wearing a gold initialed ring with the letter *J*. The cover resembled a religious tract, the kind of pamphlets I remembered seeing around the house in my childhood.

"Thank you," I said. I began to flip through the book,

glancing at the models whose eyes stared out seductively as they held cream-softened hands near their faces or suggestively touched an ear lobe.

"I've brought some things to show you," Mary Leinhart said. She took out a pearl ring and handed it to me. I could see that she was wearing the identical ring herself and, although I had no intention of buying it, I slipped it onto the index finger of my right hand. The fit was exact. I took it off quickly and handed it back.

"I do a lot of rough work," I said. "It wouldn't make it through a day with me. Tom, that's my husband, he doesn't know how to screw a lid on a mustard jar so I have to do everything that gets done around here." The floor was creaking over our heads so I knew he was in his study, pacing and smoking, passing from the files to the desk to the window. Walking, he said, helped him think, but he hated the out-of-doors, so he walked his room as other men might have walked the city.

Mary Leinhart put the ring back into its bed of cotton in a tiny box that bore a diamond design. "It's very simple and pure-looking, don't you think? I kept wondering myself how that pearl stayed on there, so I asked a jeweler. He said there's a steel pin that runs right up through the middle of the pearl. That holds it on. Now I wish he hadn't told me. I thought it was magic."

Her fingers were long, the nails shapely. They reminded me of the ads in the brochure. But she wore no nail polish and if she was wearing makeup, there was no way to tell by looking.

"These perfumes are on special this week," she said, digging into the sample case. She came up with a tray of small bottles filled with varying amounts of amber liquid. "This one's called 'Timeless.' It's my favorite." She took the cap off the bottle and handed it to me. I sniffed it, then dabbed a little onto my wrist.

"Smells like nasturtiums," I said and handed it back. It

was not a smell I liked. She didn't seem to mind, just tipped the bottle between her thumb and index finger and touched herself behind each ear. I asked to smell some others and to be told their names. I settled on one called 'Moonwind.' ''

"Do you want the perfume or the cologne?" Mary Leinhart asked.

"Perfume lasts longer, doesn't it?" I said. "I'll take the perfume."

I'd run out of places on my hands and wrists to try on more perfumes, yet I felt I should buy one more item. I pointed to a delicate necklace with three stars on it. I asked her the price and then said I'd take it.

"These face creams are very nice," she said, handing me a fat white jar with a pink label. "I have oily skin and can't use oil-based creams. This has no oil in it and it prevents lines. That's what my information says," she added.

I had trouble understanding why she was telling me about preventing lines. Surely she could see the time for that had long passed. Her own face was as line-free as a plaster-of-Paris madonna. I took the jar and dipped my fingers into it. Then I rubbed the cream onto my throat. I could feel the loose skin as I rubbed. I had what the beauty books called "turkey neck."

"Very nice," I said. I worked a little more of the cream into my forehead and remembered how it had been my sister, ten years younger than me, who had first begun to worry about my face. She'd given me an entire face-salvage kit when I was about thirty-five—complete with mud packs and eye balms. I'd even used it for a while. But it didn't take long to see that no matter what I did, a lot of things were happening anyway.

"I damaged my skin when I was in high school," Mary Leinhart said. She brushed the back of her hand across her forehead. "I had bad acne so I bought this lotion they were advertising. I'd try anything in those days. I rubbed it on and left it, like the directions said. When I washed it off, my skin was raw. Something in the formula had penetrated several layers of skin and scorched me. I had to have treatments. It left pockmarks on my forehead so I've had to put makeup there ever since. To cover it up. It's terrible what they'll try to sell you, what you'll do when you're desperate. Teenagers are always desperate about their looks. At least I was." She mused a moment, her eyes directed behind me.

Her word "scorched" stuck in my mind. She gathered up her samples. She left some catalogues on the coffee table for me to look over. We set a delivery time for the following Saturday, and I saw her as far as the front door.

I was rinsing my good cups when Tom came into the kitchen. He was helping himself to a glass of milk and wanted to know what all I'd bought from the Avon Lady and wasn't I glad I'd been home when she came, because, ha, ha, you know the stories about door-to-door saleswomen. I said I didn't know them and I didn't want to know them.

"Don't make fun of her," I said. "She's struggling. She's a nice young woman. She's had an awful time with her complexion," I said. "Someone sold her dangerous face cream when she was a kid and it scarred her face."

"I didn't see any scars," Tom said. I realized I hadn't seen any either, but I remembered feeling as though I had.

"There must have been some at one time," I said. "She covers them with makeup. She told me an awful story."

"Why are these people always coming in off the street to tell you their life stories?" he said.

"How should I know!" I said. But he was right. A chimney sweep had come to our house not long ago. He'd learned his trade in Germany, where the sweeps go to weddings and kiss all the women on the cheeks for luck.

He'd told an incredible story about falling into a well at the age of twelve. He'd had to be rescued by his father, who had lowered himself on a rope so the boy could grab onto his father's ankles and be pulled up. His affection for chimneys, he thought, was entirely due to the excitement and danger of his falling into a well when he was twelve.

Just a morning or so ago a neighbor had come over to borrow a loaf pan and had ended up telling me how their Siamese cat had rushed in behind the burning logs in the back of the fireplace and then stared back at the family through the flames. They'd had to douse the fire and the cat.

Whatever anyone said to me, I listened. Sometimes I told them back one of the stories someone else had told me. And once in a while I told it back as though it had happened to me. It was harmless enough and it gave me something to say.

We hadn't lived here long. Tom supervises the installation of computer systems in universities. We generally buy a place somewhere in the area near where he will be working and he travels short distances, two or three days out at a time. I work on the houses, and we sell them at a profit a year or so later when we're ready to move on.

A long time back I'd decided there was no use making friends when you had to pack up and leave every year. So I keep to myself. I usually get to know the guys at the local hardware store pretty well because I'm always buying insulation or paint or wiring materials from them. They give me a lot of advice and make their share of jokes, I suppose, about the old gal who's "fixing up her place." I never tell them I'm married, so they kid me, say I ought to keep an eye out for a rich widower, someone who could handle the repairs and take me on long winter vacations to Florida. I don't let on that I need anybody.

My project for the week was the repair and installation of the ground-floor storm windows. Some had panes of glass missing, others needed brackets, and still others gave no clue as to which window they belonged to. There were codes to be broken. For instance, what was I to make of KBPW? Or LRME? My success depended finally on not believing my eyes. The P of KBPW was actually an eroded R. The M of LRME was an augmented N which gave me North East. If I'd been charting our course by the stars I couldn't have been more baffled.

As Saturday approached, I began to realize I was anticipating my visit from the Avon Lady. So much so that I was disappointed to find a message Tom had left near the phone during one of my absences in search of tools or materials. "Avon Lady sick. Please call to set new time."

On the phone she sounded as if she barely had enough strength to lift the receiver. Her voice was high and girlish.

"I've got the flu. I'm running a temperature," she said. "I'll have to see you next week, if that's all right." We arranged to meet the following Saturday.

But on Saturday Tom said he needed me to drive him to a meeting in Albany. He wanted the time during the drive to review some new data before the meeting. There was no time to call Mary Leinhart. I tacked a note to the front door, saying unexpected business had come up. I felt sorry when I thought about her walking up to the door, taking down the note, reading it, and then turning and walking back down the steps.

Tom was wearing his blue suit. He smoked while he read the reports. I kept my eyes on the road and wished I could turn on the radio. It had started to rain and that seemed to make everything happen faster. Even the scenery seemed to be rushing ahead. I looked over at Tom as he turned the pages in the report. He must have felt me looking at him because he shut the folder and drew on his cigarette as he stared out the window. We were passing a truck which cut us off from the farmhouses. When we got even with the truck we could see, in modest blue lettering, "Karp's Casket Co."

"Jesus," Tom said. "Pass this guy, will you."

I tried to step on it and pull away, but we stayed even until the highway took us up a steep incline and the truck finally began to fall away behind us.

"You forget they have to make those things somewhere," he said. "Imagine, a factory where they make nothing but caskets. And the guys that work there, they have kids and when these kids get asked what their dad does they have to say, 'My dad makes caskets.'"

"And their wives," I said, "they have to say they're married to a casket-maker."

"It gives me the willies," Tom said. He lit a fresh cigarette. His brother was three years older. He'd died of a heart attack at fifty-nine just two months before. I knew Tom thought about it. He had tried to quit smoking and he tried to stop eating eggs, but he couldn't. Still, he looked trim and he liked to dress well, so that he always seemed much younger than he was. I could see the casket truck getting smaller and smaller behind us in the rearview mirror until it was a black nub in the distance.

A few days later I called the number Mary Leinhart had left with Tom and a man answered the phone. A young man. For some reason it gave me a start to hear this man's voice. I hadn't associated her with a man. I gave him the message and hung up. From time to time during the week I found myself wondering who this man was, and when Mary and I did meet that following Saturday, I said, "A man answered when I called you."

"That was my brother," she said. She unzipped one of her zippers and took out a tube of Chapstick which she rubbed across her lips. Then she zipped it back into the same slot and folded her hands on her lap. "My brother's just back from California. He's around on weekends."

"I hope you're feeling better," I said. I was sitting in the same chair as before and it seemed no time had passed since our last meeting.

"I'm better," she said. "But I've fallen behind in my school work."

"You're in school?" I said. "At the university?"

"No. The junior college," she said. "Bookkeeping. I'm not far from finishing, but I don't know if I'll ever get a chance to use what I've learned."

"Why not?" I said. I wondered if she was about to get married. Maybe there was some family problem.

"It started with my brother suggesting I have my tea leaves read," she said, raising the back of her hand to brush her forehead. "An idea he must have gotten in California. I don't usually listen to him, but he said it might be fun for me. I'd been sick. I was so far behind at school I just decided to have some fun and forget it."

She took out the purchases I'd made on her previous visit. She set them on the coffee table in a white sack with the bill neatly stapled to it. On the sack was a face, a perfect heart-shaped face of a woman representing Beauty. Under her chin was written, in slender blue script, "Open up to Beauty." It reminded me again of the urgent religious teachings of my childhood—the fundamentalist preacher at my parents' church who stood behind the altar each Sunday and said, "Open up your hearts to Jesus."

"I didn't want to go alone," Mary Leinhart said, "so I asked my sister-in-law to come with me." She took her hands out of her coat pockets. "Is it all right if I take my coat off?" she said.

"Please do," I said. It rustled as she slipped it from her shoulders and she lifted herself slightly so she could take it from behind her. She folded it once and laid it beside her, then clasped her white hands on her knees. She seemed even paler than I remembered. This made her dark eyes so prominent that I found myself staring into them. I felt I'd never looked at anyone quite in this way.

"Well, the woman told me I should develop my psychic powers," she said. She smiled, a little embarrassed to be saying such a thing. "She said I shouldn't hold back energy from these powers." There was a trace of humor in her retelling of this, but I could see she was troubled too. Suddenly she asked if I had any tea. She could use a cup of tea, she said, though she hated to put me to the trouble.

"I must still be a little weak from that flu," she said and shivered. "I was even hallucinating in the worst of it."

I said it was no trouble. I went out to the kitchen to boil the water. Tom was at a meeting with some computer hotshots from Pennsylvania and I was hoping he wouldn't get back early. It seemed important for the house to be quiet, for there to be no floor creaking above us, no other presence in the house. I fixed a little tray with napkins and took down my silver creamer and sugar bowl. I put just enough water in the kettle for two cups. When I went back into the living room with the tea I saw that she had draped her coat over her shoulders. I put the tray down in front of her and pulled my chair nearer the coffee table.

She let her tea bag stay at the bottom of her cup a long time, then danced it up and down a couple of times and took it out. She placed it on her saucer and lifted the cup to her knees, where she balanced it while she talked. They were my good china cups and they seemed exactly right for her pale, calm hands.

"The first thing the psychic said to me was: 'Who's been praying to the Virgin Mary?' Well, I'm a lapsed Catholic. I think of the Virgin sometimes but I don't pray to her, not consciously anymore. Then my sister-in-law spoke up. She said she'd been praying to the Virgin. She's very religious, so the psychic explained that's how it got into my reading. The psychic discourages anyone from sitting in on the readings. But I wouldn't have gone alone. Patty said she'd just step into the front room if she was bothering things, but I said no, if she went I went.''

She was not drinking her tea. Just warming her hands on the cup. Then she went on.

"So after we got the Virgin Mary business settled," Mary Leinhart said, "the psychic wanted to know if I'd ever seen lights. 'What kind of lights?' I asked her. 'Blue lights or sudden flashes of white lights,' she said. It's odd, but you know, I have seen lights like that off and on. When it happened I'd just been afraid, and hadn't told anyone. But once I was with someone who saw the same light. I told the psychic and she wanted to hear about it."

"Then you really believe in communications and the like?" I took a sip of my tea and waited.

"Not really," she said. She opened and closed her fingers around the cup. "This was a lark, you know, visiting the tea-leaf reader. I did want to tell her about those lights though. I admit I wanted to ask her about that."

Then she began to tell me about one particular time when she'd seen an unusual light.

"It was spring and we were looking for a place to walk that night. We wanted to be outside under the trees. I remember the trees were just getting their leaves. I remember that. There were three carloads of us. Someone thought of the cemetery, the Old Bernard Jacobs Cemetery on Nottingham Road."

As she spoke I thought I could hear people talking. The voices seemed to come from outside the house. I looked out the window behind her but I couldn't tell where the sound was coming from.

"There's a hill," Mary Leinhart said, "then a little bridge you pass over and to the right of that there's a parking area. The gate's never locked."

Then I saw where the noise was coming from. People were walking by outside, carrying their blankets and Thermos bottles. They were on the way to the basketball game. Mary Leinhart sat facing into my kitchen. She seemed to be looking into a place not in the room or even in the house.

"As I say, if I'd been the only one to see this light, I'd have been scared enough, but there was another girl—Jeannie, not someone I was especially friends with. But she saw it too. I'd gone about ten yards down the slope toward the gate when this light flashed up. It was so strong it nearly knocked me down." She drew herself back on the couch, remembering. "I turned and ran back to the car. The others came back a while later. They were laughing over near the other cars. Kind of wild. Then I noticed that Jeannie had come back ahead of them. She was inside and her face was against the car window. She looked terrible. I didn't know until later that we'd seen exactly the same light."

"Are you still cold?" I said. "Did that tea warm you or should I turn the heat on?"

"Oh, don't turn it on for me," she said. "I'll be all right. I can always put my coat back on."

"I'll just turn on the furnace a minute to take the chill off," I said.

I turned the thermostat and in a minute or two the furnace started up. Mary Leinhart had not taken anything out of her sample case. It lay on its side under the coffee table. She was still cradling her teacup in her white fingers.

"How long did that light last?" I said.

"I don't know. Several seconds. But it seemed a long time, you know. It was blinding. It seemed to be everywhere at once. It was so strong I just stood still in it and thought, 'I'm alone. I've come here alone.' That's all I remember."

"Who were these people? These people you were with?" I asked. It seemed important that she go on.

"They were friends of my ex-husband's," she said. I wanted to hear more about this husband in her past, but she went quickly on with her story.

"And then the psychic told me there was a baby in my future," she said. "She asked me if I was married and when I said no, she said then that's why I was going to be so unhappy about having the baby."

I was listening, but I couldn't avoid seeing my neighbor walking her white Samoyed out on the street. I was glad to see her. It made me feel sure I was in my house on my street. Now she was bringing the dog up onto my lawn. She was wearing her short white gloves as usual, and her high heels. They went out of sight behind a portion of wall, but I knew what was happening.

"Strangely enough, I'd been thinking sometime I might adopt a baby. By myself," Mary Leinhart continued. "That's getting easier to do now, you know. I wasn't going to do it anytime soon. 'Maybe it's my sister who's going to have a baby,' I said. Then the woman, the psychic, got angry. She stood up and threw down her shawl. 'Why does everyone want to blame things on their sisters? No, it's you, it's *your* baby,' she said."

I could see Mary was upset about the baby—that the psychic had predicted she would have it. She had to wonder how this could be so. Still her face was as calm as the faces etched on cameos, and I had to tell from her voice what she felt. She took up her coat and began unzipping the openings, looking for something.

"I have the woman's card with me," she said. "I could leave it with you if you wanted." She took out an eyebrow pencil and a circle of violet eye shadow from one pocket. From another pocket she brought out a small white stone. "There's my lucky stone!" she said. She transferred these things into her sample case.

"That's all right," I said. "If you can't find it."

I couldn't sit still. I got up and went into the kitchen. I looked around and then I brought back a plate of butterscotch cookies. I felt hungry and I thought she might be too. She took a cookie, had a small bite, then laid it next to her teacup. She had found the psychic's card and she handed it to me as I settled myself again in my chair.

"One thing the psychic said did come true," she began again. I leaned toward her and waited to hear. She took another bite of her cookie.

"The woman said I was going to be contacted. An investigator was going to come to me. She asked could I think of any instance in which this might happen. I couldn't, of course. Then last week the Board of Labor Relations sent me a letter about my last job. Some of us had filed a complaint against the boss. We'd been having to work double shifts with no breaks and the pay was below minimum. They said they were sending an investigator to talk with me. I'd forgotten all about it."

"Where had you been working?" I asked, just to keep her going.

"A place called The Blue Robin," she said. "But *there* was my investigator. Just like the woman said."

I noticed the little sack with the face of Beauty and remembered I'd ordered these things weeks before. I couldn't remember what I'd bought. I wrote out the check for the amount, and opened the sack. I took out a box. Inside was the necklace with three tiny gold stars. It was very delicate and I wanted to try it on right away. But I had on one of Tom's old shirts because I'd been painting the back steps when Mary Leinhart had arrived. I decided to wait until I was alone.

"It's just beautiful," I said. "Really, it's beautiful. It's very delicate-looking."

Mary put on her coat. She smiled at me as she buttoned it, as if we had been friends a long time.

"I'm glad you like it," she said. "Your cookies are great." She was about to leave without asking me if I wanted anything more. I picked up her catalogue and said I would take three bars of white ginger soap and a butterfly stick pin. A gift for my sister, I said.

She sat down on the edge of the couch again and got out her order blanks, then noted the catalogue prices for the soap. She apologized for having taken up so much of my day.

"I don't believe all that stuff, you know, about psychic powers," she said. "But ever since the labor investigator's letter arrived, it's been hard not to look for the other things, to wonder if they would be coming true. The baby is the one thing I can't figure. The woman said I wouldn't like it at first, but it would turn out to be the best thing in my life. I don't even have a man I care about."

I could see the idea of the baby had got hold of her. I understood how you could wish for it and not want it at the same time. I wanted to say something encouraging, but I didn't say anything. I took the slip from her and walked her to the front door. Then I opened the door and let her out. "Goodbye," I said. I watched her walk down the steps to the sidewalk. After a while I could see her blue parka and the sun striking the many zippers until she turned the corner toward James Street. I shut the door and locked it.

I went out to finish painting the back steps. I managed to pour too much turpentine into the bucket so the paint drizzled from the brush across my knee and dripped from the edges of the steps. I somehow got the paint down my arms and into my hair. I saw I'd missed the undersides of the steps and this was visible at a certain angle. I bent down and worked my way under the steps. There were places where the paint had dripped into the dirt. It was so dark under the steps I just painted by guess at first. It was like being a child, always crawling under things to see what was there. Crawling to see what it felt like to be lost, to have lost yourself from everyone.

Gradually I could see my hand above me and the paint coming out of my brush. I could see a strip of light between one step and the next.

My skin felt stiff where the paint had dropped on it. I stayed still a moment and looked out. The world was like a thought I might suddenly stop having. I closed my eyes and felt the eyelids sticking to themselves. Then I opened them when I heard someone come into the house.

I could hear footsteps in the kitchen, then the back door opening, the boards creaking on the porch. Then nothing.

"Ginny?" The voice was muffled but it was Tom's voice.

"Ginny?" he said again, and then the slat of light between the steps was blotted out as his foot came down on the wet steps. I wondered if he would see my legs. I could feel him think a moment about where I might be. I liked the smell of dirt and the darkness. By raising up on my elbow I could see the grass scuffed with white paint where he had stood, turned, then walked toward the garage. I didn't hear my name anymore. I would have to stop him before he tracked paint back into the house. The daylight made me blind a few moments as I raised myself from under the porch. When I could see again, Tom was staring at me from the side gate.

"Ginny," he said, but he wasn't calling me. "Jesus, Ginny," he said.

I knew the white paint was all over my face and arms. My eyelids were thick with it, and even though it would come off with turpentine, I could feel him hating how I looked.

"You'll have to take off your shoes," I said.

"Why didn't you answer me?" he said. He bent to

untie his shoes. I held my forearm against my brow so I could see him better. The shoes were black with white on the rims of the soles. "Didn't you hear me calling you?" he said. He held the shoes away from his suit as he walked in his socks back toward the house.

I didn't go in right away. I took a little turpentine from the can and rubbed it along my arms. I did the same to my face, holding my eyes and mouth closed. It scalded a moment as if I'd been slapped. The smell of turpentine made me light-headed. It gave little shocks to the air as I walked around to the front porch. I knocked on the door and waited to be let in.

Tom still had his shoes off. He let me in and walked ahead of me into the living room.

"I found this on the table," he said, and handed me the psychic's card. "What's this all about?"

I went past him into the kitchen and drew a glass of water. It was cool, but I thought I tasted turpentine. I put the glass aside and rubbed my mouth with the back of my hand.

"Just stick the card up on the mantel, okay?" I said. But he had followed me into the kitchen and was examining the name.

"Madame Zeller," he read aloud. "Answers your questions. Sees into your future." He tossed it onto the counter and leaned back, waiting.

"She happens to be the real thing," I said.

"I didn't know you put much stock in con artists like that," Tom said. "What do you mean, the real thing?"

"I mean she knows things. She knew things about me I haven't told anyone, not even you," I heard myself say. He was looking at me as if I had suddenly grown strange to him, let him see something that surprised him.

"And I suppose she told you the future, too," he said.

I soaked the end of a hand towel under the kitchen tap

and began to rub at my neck. I felt as if I didn't know what I might say next.

"Yes," I said. "She did. She said there would be an investigator soon. Someone checking into things." I carried the towel with me into the hall bathroom, where I got a bar of soap. My face in the mirror was smeared with a residue of white paint. I looked pale and calm.

"Investigating what?" Tom called after me.

I carried the soap with me and stood at the hall mirror, where the natural light was good.

"Just an investigation. I don't know about what. She said she could tell me, but she wouldn't. There are some things best left to the future, she said."

"It doesn't sound like you got your money's worth," he said. He was standing now in such a way that I could see him behind me in the mirror. My face was red and raw-looking in the places where I'd rubbed. He kept watching me clean myself. He wanted to question me, to find out the things that might be about to happen.

At Mercy

IN HIS OVERSIZED V-NECKED SWEATER, sitting in front of the cold fireplace, he looked like a bleak husband. She realized she'd never thought of him as a husband at all until the phone call that morning. That call had changed everything.

"Mrs. Rolland?" the voice had asked, and although she couldn't abide a lie she had said, "Yes?" She had thought the call was from the furniture people concerning delivery of the new table. But it had been one of Robert's students. For the moment of the call, she had allowed herself to be Mrs. Robert Rolland.

"I think I met you," the voice said. "Last week at the ballet."

"Oh, I don't think so," Esther had said quickly. She knew she had been in another part of the country preparing to join Robert but she asked, "What did I look like?" Her heart had begun to quaver. The voice on the other end of the line brightened.

"You were tall and your hair's reddish. Professor Rolland introduced you as his wife," the voice said. Esther had seen pictures. Robert's wife was tall and a redhead.

The rest of the day Esther had gone around the house as though it belonged to someone else. Maybe the wife had not been in town. But if she had come all the way from Idaho to Texas, certainly things were a lot less settled than Esther had imagined or than Robert had led her to believe when he told her it was over and that he wanted Esther to move into the house he'd found for them. She walked through the rooms of the house. She tried to see things with the wife's eyes. It was a big house. Certainly the wife would have known he was not planning to live here alone. She looked at the bed. She opened and closed her eyes. She could imagine them sleeping there under the patchwork quilt made by the wife's mother. She could see how, waking the last morning of the visit, the wife must have felt saddened at the prospect of suitcases and the airport. Maybe they had reached a final understanding. Or maybe the twenty-three years of Robert's marriage were not over after all, as he had assured her.

Doing anything for twenty-three years, she thought, required devotion. Her own path had been less steadfast. If anything, she had wanted too strongly for things in her own relationships to last, but when a trust was marred, she had quickly ended things. She was trying now to do otherwise, to understand, thinking of Robert and even of the wife.

In the few months they had known each other, she had thought only the best of Robert, but now that they were finally living together and he was no longer the man on the telephone who loved her, she had been trying to accommodate herself to the man himself: his smoking, the way he left food on his plate, his abruptness at meals in getting up and clearing his place before she had finished. She had tried not to care. She did little things like opening the windows and airing the rooms after he left them, pouring leftover milk from his glass back into the carton, and taking even longer at meals, making a point of enjoying her time alone at the table.

But he had been good to her since she'd arrived. The house was the biggest and most convenient house she had ever lived in. She'd never had a dishwasher and now as she portioned out the blue soap granules into the small niches in the door of the machine, then closed, locked and pressed "Full Cycle," she felt privileged and in touch with forces beyond her, forces in full control of themselves. It was a good, safe feeling.

She looked at the clock on the stove. It was two hours before Robert's class would let out and he would be home for supper. The game hens she'd taken from the freezer that morning sat stiffly in little puddles on the counter. She worked the giblets loose, rinsed the cavities under the tap, rubbed butter over the small thighs and wings with her fingers. Then she crumbled bread for the stuffing. She wondered all the while whether she should tell Robert about the phone call.

He got up from the table and moved to sit on the fireplace ledge. He folded his hands loosely between his knees. In the middle of his chest she saw the white star of his T-shirt through a cigarette hole in his brown sweater.

"Yes," he said, "she was here. Jeanette was here."

Esther leaned back on the hard rods of the rocker. She tried to remember everything Robert had promised her before she had moved in.

"She had the idea to come down with Pat," he said.

"As it turned out, I was in the hospital for the tests most of the time she was here, anyway."

"Was she coming all along? Was that why you had trouble getting my plane reservations until so late?" Robert's son, Pat, was to have visited the week before her own arrival and now she realized those plans must have included Robert's wife all along.

"No, that's not the way it was," he said. "She put me in an awful spot. She just wanted to come. At the last minute. There were a lot of things we hadn't worked out, hadn't talked about after we split up."

He did not seem to be apologizing for what he had done. She realized she wanted him to sound sorry, but he was simply matter-of-fact.

"I'd written her about you, like you wanted. Told her I'd asked you to live with me. She was upset," he said.

He wasn't looking at her. She felt she could say almost anything.

"She stayed here," Esther said. Then she said, "She slept here?"

"This might sound conceited," he said, "but I think I helped her. She was in very bad shape when she got here."

Esther wished he had sounded conceited. But he did not. He sounded like a man concerned about the well-being of someone important to him in a life she had little idea of.

"I can imagine you were a great comfort," she said, her voice high, veering. "And she was a great comfort to you. Up there in the hospital. You with an ulcer, flat on your back, not telling me where you were for days. You let her nurse you." There was an intimacy in the image of his wife standing by his bedside. She stopped herself from imagining more.

"You did this," she said, as though even his having admitted it were a way of denying it.

"Don't," he said, taking her hand into both of his. "Don't be like that. Let's not do this." She saw how his eyes were magnified under his glasses while the rest of his face looked slack.

"She didn't even have any decent clothes to wear," he said. "I took her out and bought her some clothes."

Esther cried when she heard this. She could see Robert and his wife in the lingerie section of a department store, the wife modeling a sheer nightgown and Robert looking on with approval.

"Don't you see," he said in that reasonable voice she knew men used when they wanted to make the worst things seem normal. "I'm with you." He drew her head to his face so that when she tried to turn away, she felt his tears like a scald, a wet heat as though her own face had been torn from his.

It was true, she thought. He was with her, but now so was the sense of his wife. And what was worse, they had conspired with each other against her. All his plans, he said again, were with her, Esther. They mustn't talk any more of this. It would only do damage. This mustn't be a subject they returned to. "This house is a happy house," he said, and it seemed, as he said it, that it could be true; he hadn't wanted to end things on a quarrel with his wife. He'd been thinking of the children. If he got along with his wife, surely Esther could see, surely it would be better for all of them.

He led her into the bedroom and undressed her. When they lay down, he held her with one arm under her shoulders and stroked her head, her stomach, the little dips near her collar bone. "Hold me. Hold me," she said. She felt very small and weary and his tenderness seemed sweeter than any she remembered.

In the night she woke. She thought if she read for a while she might sleep until morning. She went into the study and picked out a book of philosophy. She realized after a while that she had read the same passage uncomprehendingly several times: "Not to lie means not only refusing to hide our intentions, but also saying them and meaning them truthfully," she read. "This is not easy, and not something painlessly achieved." It seemed a message she should be able to penetrate but the words kept circling, then gliding away.

"You okay?" he asked. Robert was looking down at her through the slightly opened door. He had on his striped bathrobe, the one she had given him when he'd visited her that Christmas.

"Just reading," she said.

"Here," he said, "put this over you." He handed down an afghan to her from the linen closet in the hall. "You sure you're okay? I missed you."

Surely he was trying to be kind to everyone, she thought, and she felt she had only managed to injure him with his own goodness. She marked the page, then sat wondering how it was possible to tell for certain what you intended before you did something. What if you didn't know why you were going to do something, only that you had to do it, that you were going to do it. She carried the afghan back to bed with her and spread it over them, then crawled into his warmth.

The next day it seemed that her hope had miraculously restored itself. The sun gave sign of it, illuminating the figurine of the angel in plaster of Paris on the bureau. The folds of its robe were chipped, as were the crevices at its shoulders where the wings began. She had carried the angel since her childhood church-camp days, had even taken it to Europe with her.

Robert was cheerful. He had put on a big pot of Sanka. He still had to be careful of his ulcer, but making the

Sanka very strong gave him the feeling of drinking coffee. They had given him some pills at the hospital, and if he took these regularly four times a day the trouble would be cleared up in two months' time. Esther tried each morning to see that he ate something before he drank a second pot of Sanka.

Today he had conferences with his students and would go to his office early. She looked forward to having much of the day alone to work on her column; she had been writing a review column for *Book Weekly* for two years now, but it still took a good while for her to start the actual writing. She had learned, after some months, to fill the pages with the plots of the books and quotations, which spared her from having to reveal her opinions.

"Don't bother with dinner tonight," he told her. "We'll run away to Mexico and eat in another country." He winked and then kissed her lightly on the temple.

After he'd gathered his class folders under his arm and gone, she set up a card table near the fireplace and arranged her paper and pens, and brought out the little portable typewriter. She liked its typeface, honest and clear-hearted in its large open letters. She built a fire with juniper wood, its sweet smell making the room cozy. Like cinnamon, she thought. But even when all was ready, she could not get started. She seemed to be watching herself with the eyes of someone not altogether sympathetic.

If she could just get started, she felt it would go all right. She drew the curtains shut. She brought out several books she had read recently and chose three to review. Then she remembered the passage she'd read early that morning. As she entered the study looking for the book, she saw that one of the neighbor's cats had perched on the window ledge and was peering in at her with serious owl-eyes—scornfully, she thought. She found the book and carried it back to the card table, then opened it to the page she had turned down. The word "lie" seemed more malicious than she had experienced it before. She could not avoid the thought that Robert had lied.

The word "lie" had come to his name, and she found herself thinking again of all they had said they would not dwell on. Maybe Robert had only taken the bigger house in order to persuade his wife to come back and not at all as the place for them to begin their life together. Perhaps he had not written the wife about her at all. He might have explained away the size of the house by telling the wife he was house-sitting for someone on leave. Esther was surprised at how easily she thought of ways to sabotage her own presence. She had begun to feel sorry for the wife as someone much like herself. Someone wanting only to believe what she was told.

The fire crackled and popped. Bright chunks flew against the screen, dropped to the bricks and then turned black as they cooled. She went into the bedroom to the drawer near the telephone and took out Robert's leather address book. The wife's name was not under his last name, but she found it in the *J*'s for Jeanette. She would tell Robert she had done this, she thought, as she dialed. She felt frightened and unpredictable. A long way off a telephone was ringing while she listened.

When the woman's voice answered, Esther introduced herself, then explained hurriedly how she had discovered that she, the wife, had been there in Kingsville the week before. She said it had upset her to the degree that now she didn't know what Robert really wanted. The wife seemed very calm and assured, not the pitiable woman Robert had described who had needed new clothes, nor was she the generous-spirited woman he said had given them both her blessing. Esther had asked him just what his wife had said when he had told her he planned to live with someone else. "She said she wished us well. She hoped the best for us," he had said.

"Well you have to expect things to be difficult when you're involved with a married man," Esther heard the calm voice say. "We've been married twenty-three years and I've known him for twenty-five."

"I know," was all Esther could say. She felt helpless.

"I don't know why you're calling me," she heard the wife say. "Your relationship with Robert is your business. My relationship with him is our business."

Esther sat down on the edge of the bed and put the phone on her lap. The word "business" had brought a chill to the room. She pulled the afghan awkwardly across her shoulders. When the voice had said "ours," it had seemed to put Robert at an impossible distance.

"I'm his wife. I have a perfect right to come where he is anytime I want to. I'm the mother of his children," she said. "He asked me to come. What's more, he paid my way."

The sheer weight of the wife's insistence on her rights came down on her. She had forgotten what she had wanted of her, but she could not hang up.

"So you don't mind his living with me?" she asked.

"I didn't say that," the wife said carefully. "I said his life is his business. I just need to be alone. I don't know what Robert needs. I don't think he does either."

"Everything's fine between you and Robert then?" Esther asked.

"Yes, why? What'd he say?"

"That you had quarreled. When you left each other, I mean."

"We did no such thing. He said nothing of the kind. I just needed to be alone." The voice took strength again. "I don't know why you're talking to me. It's not very fair to Robert. I'll tell you one thing. Don't accuse Robert of lying," the voice said. "In all the years we've been together he never lied to me. I could always tell when he was telling the truth."

Esther considered this a moment, then gathered her own strength.

"This is more serious than you think," she said.

Then she hung up. She sat on the edge of the bed considering what she'd said. The way she had emphasized the word "serious" so the wife would see that she was important to Robert. Now she wondered about truth, if having the truth depended on whether or not you could tell if the person was telling it.

The angel on the bureau had attracted a pool of light. The sun passed then onto a patch of rug near the door. She saw that the angel's wings were gray and so were its hands. The more she looked at the shabby angel, the more she thought of it as irreplaceable, if only for the fact that she would never be ten years old again to paint it bright yellow. She thought of how value comes to a thing, even a thing you thought ordinary.

"At mercy," she said. "Every one of us—at mercy."

She carried the angel into the living room with her and sat down at the card table to wait for Robert. She placed it on the table so the flames from the fire caused the figurine to pause and waver like the light on her own face, making her feel at once calm and full of an unpredictable energy.

When Robert came home she waited until he had hung up his coat and put down his papers.

"I called your wife," she said. "I called her up and talked to her." Esther sounded very matter-of-fact to herself, brave almost.

Robert began to walk around the room and she could see him trying to understand why he was having to go through this.

"I don't know why you had to do that," he said. "I thought we'd settled all that." He shook a cigarette from the pack and lit it, then tossed the empty matchbook into the fireplace, where it smoldered a moment, leaped briefly with flames and burned out. Then he sat down without looking at her.

"I had to ask her some things," Esther said. "I got to thinking and I couldn't tell what to think, so I called her."

"I wish you hadn't. I wish you'd just let it alone," he said. "Now you've gone and gotten her all stirred up, too."

She hadn't expected this, hadn't thought Robert would worry about the wife now instead of trying to deal with her own concern. She looked into the fire as though the fire, for a moment, were burning quietly alone in the house with no one to tend it.

"She was fine," Esther said finally. "She wasn't exactly nice to me."

Robert looked over at her as though the workings of her mind were a complete mystery to him.

"Well what did you expect?" he asked. "Did you expect she'd be a pal?"

"You said she gave us her blessing," Esther said. "You said she wanted us to be happy. She doesn't want anything of the kind. She wants to come back anytime she pleases. She thinks she can do that. She thinks you'll let her come back." She waited a moment to see if he was going to deny this. Then she said, "I've been thinking of leaving."

Robert looked over at her and she felt that now he would see how troubled she was, how important it was that she know where she stood with him and with the wife.

"Please don't talk like that," he said. "Esther, Esther, I'm with you."

"Yes," she said, "you're with me. But your wife says she'll come here when she pleases. She says you paid her way here." It was a detail that had stuck in her mind.

"I can't tell what will happen," she said. "I got thinking maybe you should go back to your wife, that maybe she wanted you back."

"And you were just going to leave if she did?"

"I don't know," she said. "I've been feeling like nobody would tell me to do it, but that maybe I should."

"Well I'm telling you to stay," he said. He came over and stood behind her chair. She waited. It seemed to her that he waited too. Then she could feel his hands resting on her shoulders. "She won't come again," he said. "It's just us now. You and me."

They agreed not to talk about it again. She said she would stop thinking about leaving. She said she believed him. She said she knew he loved her.

But that night when she turned on her side and he pressed close and held her, his body shaping itself to hers as if it had always been so, she thought of his wife. Robert cleared his throat and rearranged his feet under the covers. She felt his breathing become deep and regular, and then she felt him pass into sleep. But her eyes were open. She could see their shoes lined up under the dresser. For some reason they reminded her of small boats at anchor. She lay with his arm around her and thought of the time she had seen a group of friends off on a cruise, waving until the ship pushed away from the dock and moved steadily into deeper waters. He brought his knees up into the space behind her knees and held them there. She kept thinking of the ship and it was as though she were on board. She was aware of the other passengers sleeping. Waves slapped against the hull. She lay still and felt the throbbing, the small steady tremors of engines.

A Pair of Glasses

HER GRANDMOTHER WOULD PUT ON GLASSES to read labels on cans when the girl went to the market with her. The grandmother would read the brand names and the prices out loud to the girl. The girl could not read much yet herself, but sometimes she pretended she could. The grandmother would read a word, and the girl would say it to herself and stare at the word—trying to hold it in her mind. They would go down the aisles this way, the girl pushing the cart and saying the brand names and prices. At the counter the grandmother would take her billfold out of her purse, hand the purse to the girl and take off the glasses.

"Here, put these away for me, honey," she'd say, and

the eyeglasses would come into the girl's hands. It was always an important moment, to be holding the glasses. Under the lenses the girl's fingers seemed larger, and as if they had a life of their own. When she looked down, her shoes leapt up at her from the floor. Once when her grandmother had to leave the counter for a moment, the girl had put the purse in the shopping basket and opened up the eyeglasses. She set them on the bridge of her nose and held them there, looking around at the blurred faces of the other shoppers. It was a wonderful, dizzying feeling and it gave her the idea that the wearing of glasses was a way of seeing that only a few people were privileged to have. When the grandmother returned with the missing grocery item, she took the eyeglasses from the girl.

"You're going to break those, honey. Here, let's put them away." Then the glasses had gone back inside the purse until the next shopping trip.

Neither the girl's father nor her mother wore eyeglasses. The nearest thing to glasses in the house was a pair of field glasses her father kept in the corner cabinet. He used these when he went deer hunting and also to watch ships passing through the inlet of water which their house faced. Once the girl had stood in a chair at the window and her father had stood behind her holding the field glasses to her eyes. The glasses were heavy.

"Can you see now?" he asked her. He twisted the lenses and the girl stared into the glasses until she could begin to see an object taking shape. When she could tell what it was, she jumped up in the chair until her nose knocked against the metal bridge of the glasses.

"A boat! A boat with a man in it," she reported. Then her father said sternly, "Now you're getting silly. Stand still or I'll put them away." Then the girl stood still and watched the waves lapping the side of the boat. The man stood up and turned sideways so the girl could see he was reeling on a fishing pole.

"He's got a fish!" the girl said, pressing her eyes into the metal rims of the field glasses.

"Let me see," her father said, and lifted the glasses from her. Then she could see only a far black speck on the blue-gray water.

"I don't think he's got anything," her father said after he'd held the glasses on the speck a long time. "If he did, he lost it." Finally her father put the glasses back into their leather case.

The girl liked the smell of the leather case. Sometimes she would beg to be allowed to put the field glasses away, just for the pleasure of how perfectly the lenses slid into the darkness of the case. Then she snapped the case shut and her father swung the glasses up to the top of the corner cabinet, until the next time he wanted to watch something on the water.

No one in the girl's class at school wore eyeglasses, but on the playground she saw several children who did wear them. This set them apart from the others—as if they might be smarter or able to see things she couldn't. She began to yearn for the company of those who wore glasses.

At recess the girl played jump-rope with an older girl who wore glasses. The other girl's name was Brenda, and Brenda loved to jump double-dutch. The girl was especially good at turning the ropes for double-dutch, so Brenda often asked her to get a partner and turn the ropes while she jumped. Besides the glasses, which had blue plastic rims, Brenda had pigtails which her mother often tied with blue ribbons. The girl thought the sight of Brenda jumping double-dutch with her blue-rimmed glasses and the blue hair-ribbons bouncing on her pigtails between the whipping sound of the ropes was the most wonderful sight she could imagine.

Then one day while the girl was turning the ropes, one of Brenda's pigtails caught in the ropes and the blue-rimmed glasses went flying. The girl dropped her end of the ropes and ran over to the glasses before anyone else could reach them. She picked them up. But when she saw the crack across one lens she started to cry. Brenda was upset too and the girls wept into each other's hair with the eyeglasses pressed between them. The next day Brenda came to school without the glasses and she seemed then, to the girl, to have passed back into the ranks of the ordinary.

It was late October and leaves covered the sidewalk. The girl walked to school in the crisp morning air. On her way she gathered a bouquet of the brightest orange and red leaves she could find. She gave these to her teacher, Miss Binki. Miss Binki was very tall and slender, but one feature of her appearance held the girl's amazement, and she supposed that all the other students were similarly fascinated. Miss Binki had pointed breasts that pushed her sweater out. The girl stared with her mouth open as the breasts moved around the schoolroom, hovering over her classmates' shoulders when Miss Binki stooped beside them to help with their work. Some days the breasts seemed more prominent than others. These were days when Miss Binki apparently felt like setting a good example for her students. It was then she would show them how to stand tall and straight with their shoulders back and chests out. Good posture was important, Miss Binki said, and Miss Binki saw to it that they practiced it by walking around the room with encyclopedias balanced on their heads.

The girl carried the volume *Bu–Cz* on her head. When she passed Miss Binki's desk the woman smiled at her. It was at this minute the girl lost her balance and the book tumbled from her head across Miss Binki's desk and into her lap. Miss Binki very calmly picked up the book, walked around the desk and placed it back on the girl's head. After a moment, the girl continued walking.

Once, before leaving for school in the morning, the girl asked her mother if there wasn't something she could take to Miss Binki as a present. Her mother went into the fruit cellar and brought up a jar of raspberry jam. The girl carried the jam to school and placed it on Miss Binki's desk before the teacher arrived.

"Who brought me this nice jar of jam?" Miss Binki asked the class once they were all seated at their desks. The girl was too shy to answer. Then one of the boys who'd seen the girl put the jam on the desk began to point his finger and call, "She did, she did!" Later, on the playground, this same boy called her "teacher's pet" and chanted this until the girl left the playground.

It was about this time that the girl, in the presence of grown-ups, began to rub at her eyes with the heel of her hand and to blink when the grown-ups talked to her. At school the children were cutting out pilgrims—the men in their tall black hats, the women in bonnets. The girl preferred to draw. She drew a turkey with a tail showing all the colors in the rainbow. She drew a pilgrim holding the turkey by the feet, and she added a pair of spectacles to the pilgrim. She told Miss Binki that this was so he could see all the beautiful colors of the tail feathers. But in the girl's reading group she complained that she couldn't see the letters plainly, and she asked to be moved closer to the blackboard.

Miss Binki sent a note home with the girl in a sealed envelope. Not long after that, the girl's father and mother dressed up in their good clothes and drove the girl to an eye doctor for an examination. At first the girl thought this doctor must be a kind of dentist and that he intended to pull her eyes out. She put her fists over her eyes and braced against the wall of the office. She wouldn't go into the examination room. But finally she took her father's hand and went into the room, which held various machines and charts. After a short while, the doctor came in. The girl noticed that he was wearing a pair of spectacles himself, and then that he was wearing a white jacket with several pens clipped to his pocket. The doctor turned off the lights in the room and positioned himself in front of the girl. He began to flash sharp pinpoints of light into her open eyes. Then he asked her if she knew the alphabet. The girl said she did. The doctor began to project different-sized letters of the alphabet onto a large screen on one wall of the examination room. The girl knew something serious was taking place. Her parents were worried about her eyesight. They had brought her to a man who gave out eyeglasses to those with poor eyesight. The girl hoped more than anything that her eyesight would be found poor enough so the doctor would prescribe a pair of eyeglasses for her.

When the letter *C* flashed onto the screen the girl knew it was *C,* but she said "*O.*" An *h* appeared and she said it was a *b*. If there was an open space to the letter, she closed it and made another letter out of it. Sometimes she couldn't think what to do, so she just said she couldn't see what the letter was. She was certain she'd demonstrated that she had terrible eyesight. Leaving the examination room, she bumped into things as the bright daylight streamed down on her.

She sat with her mother in the waiting room while the doctor talked to her father. Finally her father came out.

"You talk to him," her father said to her mother.

Then the girl sat with her father until her mother reappeared. Her mother was nodding to what the doctor was saying. "We'll talk it over," her mother told the doctor. "We'll see."

The girl felt worried and happy at the same time. She

got into the car with her parents and stared out the window as they passed all the familiar stores and houses of the town. When they arrived home her parents went inside and into the kitchen, where they made coffee and sat at the kitchen table. They were quiet and the girl supposed they were thinking of what to do about her bad eyes. She wondered why they hadn't had her fitted for eyeglasses right then and there at the doctor's office— why she was being allowed to walk around in such a condition. Then her father called her over to the table and told her to sit with them.

"The doctor says you've got an eye disease," her father said. "It could get worse, and it could get better. But there are treatments, and if that doesn't work there's an operation they can do." Her father looked at her mother and then took a sip from his coffee. "But it costs a lot of money," he said. "There's no way we can pay for such things," her father said.

"Here, honey," her mother said. "Here's a glass of milk. Sit over here next to me and drink it." The girl moved over next to her mother, took the glass of milk and looked into it as if it had betrayed her. She felt too sad to drink anything, but she took several large gulps of milk.

"We'll just have to hope the trouble isn't as serious as the doctor thinks," her mother said. "Maybe it will clear up."

In the days and weeks that followed, the girl tried to remember that she had bad eyes, but she often forgot and became perfectly able to see words on the blackboard. Miss Binki praised her and several times said how glad she was that the girl's eyesight was improving. This forgetfulness did not mean that the girl had given up the idea of getting her own pair of glasses.

On a trip to the dimestore with her grandmother to buy

hair ribbons, the girl had spotted rows and rows of eyeglasses between the handkerchief and yarn displays. When she picked up a pair and peered through them, the shelves in the store had loomed up around her until the pit of her stomach ached. She begged her grandmother to buy her a pair.

"Those glasses are for old people like me," her grandmother said. "Those are reading glasses for very weak, tired eyes like mine."

A few days before Christmas the girl's father asked her to name a few things she might like to find under the Christmas tree when she opened her gifts.

"A pair of glasses," the girl said. "Like those in the dimestore."

"Oh, I don't know about that," her father said and laughed. Then he looked at her and said, "Is that what you really want?"

"Yes," the girl said. "A pair of eyeglasses."

On Christmas Eve the girl opened her gifts with her parents and grandmother watching. She got a pair of rain boots, more hair ribbons and a bag of peppermint candies. But no eyeglasses. Then her father left the room and came back with a small package.

"Here," he said. "Maybe this will cheer you up."

Inside the wrapping paper was a pair of eyeglasses from the dimestore. The girl was so happy she forgot all her other gifts. She unfolded the eyeglasses and tried them on.

"They're a little big," her mother said. "Maybe we should take them back and get a smaller pair."

"No, no," the girl cried. "They fit me. They fit fine." She got up from the chair she'd been sitting in and took a few steps into the room. The glasses wiggled on her nose as she walked, and the room seemed to tilt back and forth. The Christmas tree lights blurred into each other and blazed against her face as she stared at them. The faces of her parents and her grandmother seemed odd to her, like masks, and she drew back from this vision. But mostly she was pleased with what she saw when she looked out through the eyeglasses. She felt as if she had grown larger, and although she knew this wasn't so, she loved the feeling because she thought it made her seem older.

The next day she wore the glasses all day. She was disappointed that there were no children in the neighborhood she could show them to. School would begin again in a few days, she knew, but in the meantime she was the only one except her family who knew she had a pair of eyeglasses. That evening, her mother came in to say good night and discovered the girl in bed with her glasses on.

"What do you expect to see while you're asleep?" her mother asked, and took the glasses from her. But the next day her mother gave them back. The girl put them on when the mailman came. She met him on the porch.

"Are you the doctor of the house?" he asked. "Oh no, you're the professor. Here's some mail to answer," he said. The girl came back into the house carrying the mail and feeling very proud because the mailman had noticed that she had her own pair of eyeglasses.

School was starting again after the Christmas vacation, and the girl's father said to her that morning, "Now have a little sense, honey. Don't take those glasses to school." So the girl had been all day at school without her eyeglasses. She ran all the way home after school and hurried into the house. She found the eyeglasses in the drawer of her nightstand where she'd put them for safekeeping. She spit onto each of the lenses and then polished them with the hem of her skirt. She put the glasses on and went out into the yard to lie on her back and stare up at the clouds. But the sky was so bright she closed her eyes and daydreamed instead.

The next day she slipped the eyeglasses into her lunch bucket and took them to school. She sat in her seat in Miss Binki's class and put them on. She felt very special and different from the other children as she sat with her glasses on. It did not matter that she could hardly see to write her name at the top of her paper. She was happy and proud to be wearing eyeglasses.

Miss Binki kept looking in the girl's direction, and the girl supposed that Miss Binki was admiring her glasses. Then Miss Binki came up beside the girl's desk and spoke to her.

"Did you get a new pair of glasses?" Miss Binki asked. "Are your eyes bothering you again, dear?"

"Yes," the girl said. "I got some glasses for Christmas."

"May I see them?" Miss Binki asked.

The girl did not hesitate. She wanted Miss Binki to admire her glasses. She handed them up to her and watched Miss Binki try them on.

"Oh my! Oh dear," Miss Binki said. "Your eyes can't be *this* bad. You're going to ruin your eyes, dear, wearing these glasses." Miss Binki removed the brown-rimmed glasses from her nose and slipped them into her dress pocket. Then she took a step away. The girl could not believe what was happening. She sat gazing at the pocket into which her glasses had disappeared.

"I'll save them for you," Miss Binki said. "You can have them back at the end of the year." She walked to her desk and the girl saw her take the eyeglasses out and place them into her desk drawer and turn a key. It was a drawer into which the girl had seen many forbidden items disappear. Things of an altogether different nature from her eyeglasses—a succession of slingshots, marbles, toys, candy bars—all to be collected by their owners at the end of the school year.

The girl went home in tears. She told her mother and father what had happened. She thought surely they would go to Miss Binki and get her eyeglasses back. But the girl's father only shook his head and said, "It's good enough for you. I guess you'll learn to listen now."

After that the girl had periods where she forgot entirely about the glasses. But there were other times when she would fasten her attention on them there in Miss Binki's desk drawer, and she would be unable to think of anything else. She knew that the end of school was months away.

The girl's opinion of Miss Binki began to change. She no longer seemed the beautiful young woman all the children loved for her pointed breasts and bright red lipstick. The girl had noticed something decidedly sharp, even harsh, about the woman's features. There were lines under her eyes. Miss Binki called for quiet more and more often. Several times a day children were banished to the cloakroom for misbehaving. But the girl continued to conduct herself quietly and patiently in the hope that she would do nothing further to bring disfavor to herself.

Finally it had come, the last day of school, and the children were told to form a line at Miss Binki's desk. She was handing back the last of their schoolwork. It was also the moment at which the children who'd had their belongings appropriated would have them returned. The girl was fully prepared to forgive Miss Binki when her eyeglasses were returned to her. She was thinking this, that she would apologize, when suddenly her turn came and she found herself standing before Miss Binki. The teacher had put on her best posture for these final moments at her desk with her students. Her head was erect and her back was straight.

"Here you are, dear," Miss Binki said, handing the girl the bundle of drawings and scribblings. She smiled at the girl. "Have a good summer."

"My glasses," the girl said.

"I knew there was something," Miss Binki said. "But I almost forgot." She reached into her desk drawer and brought out the eyeglasses. "Yes, here are your glasses. I don't think they'll hurt your eyes now. You have a good summer, dear."

The girl took the glasses and ran with them out into the schoolyard. She dropped her papers and fitted the eyeglasses to her head. But something was wrong. The world stayed the same. There was no miraculous fuzziness and the girl felt the same as she'd always felt—too small and too young. Her stomach did not leap and swerve with each step she took. Her glasses had somehow lost their magic in Miss Binki's desk drawer. The girl put her hand up to touch the lenses and was surprised when her finger went through the frame into her eye. She gave a little cry and took off the glasses. Then she saw that the lenses had been removed from the frames. The girl held the glasses and stuck her finger through the frame into one of the eye spaces and twirled the eyeglasses in disbelief. Then she put the glasses back on to make sure. She could see other children coming gaily in little groups out of the school building. She saw her papers blowing crazily across the schoolyard. She was seeing with her own good eyes through the plastic rims.

There was a tight feeling in her chest as she walked slowly home wearing the empty frames. There were moments when her eyes welled up, and it seemed that the lenses had miraculously returned to the glasses. But when she reached her fingers up through the rims and wiped her eyes, she found she could see quite normally. She thought of Miss Binki bent over her eyeglasses, purposely removing the lenses. As she imagined this, a hot feeling came up in her. It was a feeling so terrible that the girl stopped where she was on the sidewalk and shouted, "I hate her! I hate her!" A man who was sitting with his dog on his front porch looked at her and the girl felt the awful feeling pour out of her until she became afraid and began to run as fast as she could, holding the eyeglass frames to her face with one hand.

When the girl reached home she didn't go into the house but went instead around to the backyard and sat in the swing. She kicked herself high into the air in the swing, then higher, until she felt she might fly out over the rooftops. Gradually the feeling of hatred left her. After a while she climbed down from the swing and went into the house for supper.

"What did I tell you," her father said at the supper table. The empty frames lay near her plate. "I guess that serves you right, doesn't it," her father said.

"Even if the teacher meant well—and I'm sure she did," her mother said, "it was a mean thing to do." The girl's mother went to the stove and took up the rest of the fried potatoes. But the girl knew her mother couldn't understand.

The girl didn't say anything. She chewed her food slowly and felt she had fallen into the company of people who hated eyeglasses. She didn't know why this was so. She squinted at her plate. It seemed a great effort to lift food to her mouth. She was glad when at last her plate was empty.

The Woman Who Saved Jesse James

I<small>T WAS MID-AFTERNOON BY THE TIME</small> I'd settled into my room at the resort. My friends wouldn't arrive until the following day. Every three years several women I'd been with at cooking school twenty years ago would join me for a few days' vacation. We always had such a good time we wondered why we didn't do it every summer. But the other women had husbands and families or summer retreats of their own, so we settled for meeting every three years.

I'd decided to come a day early and answer a few letters. This was not as easy as it sounds, because some of the letters were at least five years old. I work at home, compiling cookbooks with titles like *Frozen Bread, Coffee*

Cake Bonanzas or *Appetizers Galore*. Everything falls by the wayside, especially mail, when I'm collecting recipes and testing them. Macy, the woman who works with me testing the recipes, also does some of my filing. That's how these five-year-old letters came to the surface. Macy had come across them in a box where I keep photo albums—pictures of ex-husbands with my ex-selves and ex-parents-in-law, and the forgotten friends of ex-in-laws.

"Why don't you just chuck them out if you're not going to answer them?" Macy had asked me one day. I'd caught her with the box tipped toward the trash barrel.

Macy's right, of course. Who are these neglected writers anyway? Are they worth bothering with if they don't even complain? Still, I'd carried the box back into the house and made myself open a few of the envelopes. I skimmed over questions about people who'd long since left my life, or otherwise ceased to be of concern. People who now lived happily or unhappily in faraway cities, in other countries even. Some of the letters carried bad news from which the writers had probably recovered long ago. Or hadn't. Others wanted to share a triumph—a new job, or a child, the purchase of a car.

There was a mixture of regret and pleasure in rereading these letters. Mostly I felt regret. I sat with the letters and felt older, as though I'd fallen behind myself. Trying to answer the letters seemed a way of catching up, of saving what I'd had to let go. That's when I got the idea of coming to the lake a day early and trying to answer the people who'd assuredly given up on me.

I arranged my things in the cabin, then carried the typewriter to a picnic table near the edge of the lake. I held the folder of letters and my stationery under one arm. There was a breeze from the lake, so I looked for something to put on the stationery to hold it down. I found a rock about the size of my hand and walked back to the table. There were a few water-skiers buzzing back and forth on the lake. The shadows from the hills would close over the lake before long, the skiers would get cold and go in.

I rolled a piece of blue stationery into the typewriter and looked out along the lake again. Two boys with one fishing rod between them were trying for something. The one with the rod was casting from the dock, taking direction from the other boy. But in no time the boy had snagged the branch of a downed tree that jutted from the water several yards from shore. After a while I could see him sloshing up to his waist, tugging on the line.

I decided to make some rules for myself. I would take each letter only in the order it came to me as I reached into the folder. I would have to answer in that order. I could draw two at a time.

I put my hand into the folder and took out the first letter. The postmark told me it was over three years old. I didn't recognize the name on the return address, which was from Dallas. I hoped the letter would give me a clue so I'd have something to say. I drew a second letter. It was from a woman I'd worked with at the Sheraton Hotel in Denver. I'd cooked there fifteen years ago. Dotty Mayfair was her name. The letter was only a year old and had been written from Sugar Grove, Wyoming. I seemed to remember that it concerned her having remarried and settled down in Wyoming to run her own cooking service which catered to ranches in the area. "Gone to biscuits," I'd said to myself when I'd read that. I'd remembered her for her baked Alaskas and cherry cheesecakes during our hotel days.

I wanted to break my rules right then and answer Dotty first. Then I saw that the first letter had never been opened. Somehow it had made its way into the unanswered folder without ever having been read. I looked up as I tore it open, in time to see the boy with the fishing

rod dive into the water and swim out toward the limb.
The other boy was holding the rod. The head of the swim-
mer bobbed toward the branch.

The letter was handwritten in a cramped script, but the
words were legible. The gist of it was that the writer, a
Jim Danzer, wanted to hear from me. What had become
of me since I'd left Dallas and the Sutter's Mill Steak
House? Had I found a man to suit me? Then came a long
story about his mother's illness. He'd been attending to
that or he would have written sooner. He was still going
into Sutter's asking for pie as good as my cherry-apple
pie. Good, I thought. Good for him. If I was ever passing
through I was to let him know. In the meantime, it was
possible he might be coming my way—in about two
weeks. He would not force his attentions on me, but
would wait to hear whether it was okay to stop for a visit.

When I looked up, the boy had reached the snarled
line and was shouting to his friend, "Give me some
slack!" The boy on shore began to spool line from the tip
of the rod and loop it into the water.

I tried to remember Jim Danzer. He used to sit alone in
a booth on a Saturday night, a never-married-but-still-
looking cattle rancher who came into the city on business
every so often. I'd talked with him more than once, may
even have met the mother he mentioned. I couldn't re-
member. In any case, we'd missed our chance.

I looked at the page of stationery rolled into my type-
writer. Then glanced to the far side of the lake, the sum-
merhouses and boat docks. I thought about Dotty getting
a letter from me out in Wyoming. Maybe she'd have to
drive to a main road where the mailboxes for an entire
area would be lined up with names scrawled on their
sides. Or maybe one of those rural drivers in a pickup
would turn in at the ranch house and honk for her to
come out. She'd have on her apron. She'd be wearing a
hairnet which she'd pull off before she opened the door. I

remember how she hated for a man to see her in that hairnet.

She was a good woman, Dotty. She was always taking up collections for people's birthdays at work or, if they were sick, getting together some little gift item and card for them. Our connection, at the time we'd worked together, centered around a woman named Miss Nix. This woman was a retired English teacher, though her life had gone downhill so badly no one would have guessed. She had multiple sclerosis. Dotty had been going over to make her lunch every day—this on top of her regular cooking shift. Oh, she got paid, but not enough to make it worthwhile that way. I used to spell Dotty on her job at the hotel so she could make the run over to Miss Nix's place and get back in time to cook the dinner specials. When Dotty quit her job at the hotel and decided to go West, I inherited Miss Nix. It was a depressing thing to have right there in the middle of the day. In the beginning I didn't know if I'd last the week.

I adjusted the paper in my typewriter and wondered if Dotty ever gave a backward thought to Miss Nix. I remembered the time Dotty had come to work a Kiwanis Club luncheon with me. She started in complaining—the lettuce, she said, must have been lying in the sun for a week. Where *did* they get that lettuce! But I knew something more than lettuce was wrong. Finally it came out. Dotty had just come back from Miss Nix's, where she'd opened a can of protein mix for her. Miss Nix lived on this sweet-smelling, cream-colored stuff. She used to go through a case of it every two weeks. But when Dotty got there that day, she'd found Miss Nix in tears. Miss Nix wouldn't touch the junk after Dotty opened the can and poured it into a tall glass for her. She told Dotty twelve of her best friends had died that month. "Imagine that," Dotty had said when she told me, "to lose a dozen friends in that short a time. The poor old dear."

I heard about those twelve friends too—after I started to work in Dotty's stead. At the time, it made me think that I didn't have six close friends to lose, let alone a dozen. It was plain to see that Miss Nix must have had another life before she'd ended up bedridden, watching TV serials and reading the *National Enquirer*.

I'd confessed to Dotty that I didn't see how she'd gotten herself into the business with Miss Nix in the first place. Miss Nix ought to be in a nursing home, I told Dotty. "Well now, Lorna, you're probably right," Dotty had said. "I know you're right. Anyone would agree with you. But I can see myself in her place, helpless, and everybody ready to ship me off. It's then I want her to be left alone, just left right where she is." I never said any more about it to her after that.

If I wrote to Dotty I could start by asking after her health. In those days she'd had bursitis in her shoulders, and when the weather changed she used to complain about the soreness. My own health has always been excellent. I never thought much about getting old and infirm until I started working for Miss Nix. Once Dotty and I gave her a bath—Dotty holding her by her shoulders in the tub so she wouldn't slip down. I still remember what Miss Nix's skin felt like. It was loose on her bones when I rubbed her—loose the way chicken skin is when you rub butter on it. When I got home that night and took my own bath, I had this sensation as if I was melting away right inside my skin. I got out of the tub and stood in front of a full-length mirror to look at myself. I took hold of the skin on my abdomen and pulled on it. Then I checked my breasts. I thought of getting old—old like Miss Nix. I put my clothes on right away, and some lipstick. Then I fixed myself a drink.

It wasn't long afterwards that Miss Nix pointed her finger at me and, for no reason I could fathom, said there'd come a time when I'd look back and know what it was to need people. "Even people who don't love you. People who don't give a damn," she'd said. "You're strong now, you've got the world by the tail. But the years will come down on you. Mark my words." Then she'd had me light her cigarette and change the TV channel for her.

There were good times with Miss Nix, too. Times when you wondered how she'd washed up there alone. She was spunky in the mornings, before she ran out of steam. She'd tell stories about growing up in Missouri. One story I remember had to do with Jesse James. It seems Jesse had been on the run from the law and had knocked on the door of the farmhouse where Miss Nix was a baby. She had colic and her mother was rocking her. Her father was off somewhere with the cattle. "Give me the baby," Jesse James had told the mother. So Miss Nix was handed over to the outlaw. The mother was terrified, of course, and she didn't even know it *was* Jesse James. She was a woman alone and there was nothing she could do.

"Jesse James began to pace up and down with me," Miss Nix said. "My mother said he held me right up close to his face."

When the sheriff arrived, he pushed his way into the house—looking for Jesse James, he said. That's when the mother knew who was holding her child. But all the sheriff saw was a father and a mother looking after their colicky baby.

"The sheriff just stood there. I was the only disguise Jesse needed," Miss Nix said. "My mother said I did my part. I cried and cried. Finally the sheriff couldn't stand the noise and left." Then Miss Nix told how Jesse James helped himself to a cup of beans from the pot on the stove. Then he'd borrowed a cow to lead down the road to the neighbors. If the sheriff happened to double back, Jesse would be disguised by the cow. He would look like a farmer.

"He walked the cow to our neighbor," Miss Nix said. "Then he bought a horse from that man. Paid good money. Then I guess he rode on to join up with his gang, and to continue robbing banks and trains. But I'm the woman that saved Jesse James that day."

After Miss Nix told this story I'd sometimes catch myself thinking, "That's the woman that saved Jesse James."

The wind was getting up on the lake. I'd only gotten as far with my letter as "Dear Dotty." There was no sign of the water-skiers now—only a thin rim of sunlight on the far side of the lake.

If I was going to write Dotty at all, it had to be about something that mattered, I decided. I didn't know exactly why Miss Nix mattered, but I felt she did. You can't know how you're going to end up in this life. Miss Nix was the living proof of that. One day when I was over there I'd come across a photograph of her in her college graduation gown, and I realized that the smiling young woman on the front lawn was the same woman who could now barely lift a spoon to her mouth.

The story I wanted to tell Dotty had to do with an alcoholic named John who used to come around to Miss Nix's to run a few errands for her. She would give him money and sometimes they'd watch TV together. He was a good twenty years younger than Miss Nix. In his fifties maybe.

I hadn't been working more than a month for Miss Nix when I went over there one day and found the bedroom thick with cigarette smoke. Miss Nix was in bed staring out the window. She wouldn't even look at me. I took off my coat. "What's wrong?" I asked her.

"He got in here with me," she said finally, and then she put her head on her arms and started to cry.

"He who?" I asked, but somehow I knew she meant John. "John?"

But she wouldn't say his name. She just nodded into her arms and kept moaning.

I felt terrible. I wanted to do something. Kick something or yell. But I just got up and took a cigarette from her pack and sat down again. The face of the young girl in her graduation gown crossed my mind, and I thought of Miss Nix with that tassel hanging over one eye.

"I'm seventy-two years old," Miss Nix said. "You'd think it would be too late for that. You'd think I could have got off this earth without that."

I just sat there like a stump, watching some hydroplanes churn and spout across the TV screen. "I think you ought to tell the police," I said.

She clammed up. She didn't want to talk about police. "Close the screen, but leave the door open," she told me, when she saw I was getting ready to leave. I knew better than to argue with her. After all, it was her house. "You sure you don't want the door locked?" I asked. She was sitting up in bed, smoking a cigarette. "The damage is done," she said, without turning her head. The smoke curled up from the hard tips of her fingers. It didn't seem right to leave her like that, but I did. I closed the screen and left.

Later that night I got to thinking about Miss Nix all alone there in the house. I was worried that John would show up again. I was no relation to her, but I was up to my neck in her situation. I decided to call Clara Zimmer, the woman who'd worked for Miss Nix before Dotty had. I wanted to see what she knew about John.

I told Clara over the phone what had happened, and Clara started to laugh. I told her I didn't think it was a laughing matter.

"I'm sorry," Clara said. "But Lorna, that woman is crazy as a loon. I'm surprised Dotty didn't warn you."

"Warn me about what?" I said.

"About John the rapist. Miss Nix is making that up,"

Clara said. "It's happening all right, but it's happening in her head."

I was dumbfounded. Like when people claim women want it when these things happen. Then it made me mad. But at the same time I'd seen old people, some of them running on half a battery, confused, stuck in some moment that had happened long ago or never happened at all. Cooking is easy compared to figuring out things like that. You add ingredients in the required amounts. You do it in the given order at the right temperature for the right amount of time. You follow directions and you get results. Motives and truth have nothing to do with a good dish. If something goes wrong you can usually find the reason. You can even throw it out and start over.

A week went by. I drove over to Miss Nix's every chance I had, sometimes twice a day. I was living with this French Canadian man at the time, and he was getting fed up.

One night he said, "Why the hell don't you just pack up and move in with her if she's so damned important."

"Maybe I will," I said. "You'd better hope somebody cares about you when you're sick and can't do for yourself." The words were hardly out of my mouth when I realized he'd be done with me in a minute if I ever got disabled. We had a big blowout that night. He said he wanted me to go back to Quebec City with him, meet his friends, have a vacation. How'd he think we were going to get there, I wanted to know. I was working two jobs to pay the bills and whose money, I asked him, were we going on? I was tired of taking orders from him. Then he got rough with me, and I had to hightail it to my sister's place in Glendale. I cut my losses, and the long and short of it is that Miss Nix fell by the wayside. That was the last I saw of her. I don't know what happened to her after that. I'd cut the anchor rope and left her to get through her days as best she could.

I was sitting there in front of the typewriter. But I wasn't writing anything. I looked up and saw the resort manager. He was calling and motioning to me from his office door.

"Long dis-tance, Miss Parker," he shouted. I got up and hurried toward the office. When I got to the desk, the manager went over to a file cabinet and started to shuffle some paper like he was too busy to leave the room. He wanted to listen.

It was Macy. She had a message from Jane Peterson, one of my friends. Jane needed a lift from the airport. She'd decided to fly to a nearby town rather than drive up. She'd be in tomorrow afternoon. The manager smiled when I hung up. He was Middle Eastern and his smile was broad.

"No trouble," he said. "Always glad any time good news."

When I got back to my typewriter I saw that the wind had swept the letters over the grass. Some had gusted into the lake and were floating away like small white birds. The letter from Dotty was nowhere in sight.

I gathered up the envelopes I could catch and stuffed them back into the folder. I was mad at myself for not fastening the letters down. Yet in a way I was glad too, as I watched them being pulled further and further from shore. I took the page with "Dear Dotty" typed on it out of the typewriter. Then I found a pen in my letter box and thought a minute of Dotty. It was as if she'd been sitting there all afternoon listening to me. I was ashamed I hadn't done more for Miss Nix. I felt Dotty would have stuck by her. But maybe not. Dotty was out in Wyoming with a new husband. She wasn't thinking about Miss Nix. She was doing what she had to do to look out for herself. I reached into my pocket file of new recipes and selected a few to put into the envelope. "Try these and think of me," I wrote across the page to Dotty. Then I considered how I should sign it. I wrote "Love," then signed my name. I folded it in with the recipes and wrote Dotty's maiden name on the envelope, along with Sugar Grove, Wyoming. I had to hope it would get to her.

I thought of my friends who would arrive the next day. We'd sit by the lake and exchange recipes. We would all be a little fatter and a little older. One of the women was an expert on sauces. Another was a gourmet health-food cook, and a third had recently been to India and Pakistan to study the dishes there. We would have dinners out in the nearby villages and we'd probably get a little drunk and sing by the lake after dark. Yet I knew that not one of these women would nurse one of the others if she were to fall ill and had no one to look after her. It made me sad to know this—though I couldn't claim to be any different myself, if it got right down to it. That was the hard part. Knowing that.

Miss Nix was the only person I'd ever taken care of. At the time, everybody at work had said what a good thing I was doing. What a blessing I must be to that poor old woman. But all along I'd felt they weren't talking about me, only finding a way to show how glad they were it wasn't them having to wait on Miss Nix hand and foot. "The poor old dear," they would say. "She ought to thank her lucky stars for you. Someone to look after her in her last days." But I knew I was just another Jesse James in her life. Ready to walk in and out the same door. I'd left her at the mercy of John and whoever else would come along before her money ran out. I'd been no better than a common bandit, though everybody thought I was the Good Samaritan.

I felt mean and pinched to admit all this to myself. But what could I have done, under the circumstances? Jesse James couldn't have stayed on there at the farmhouse pretending to be a father. He had a getaway to make. I couldn't imagine he ever gave that day a backward glance, that woman alone with a colicky baby. He'd gotten away and what he did after that was his business. Miss Nix would have been the first to say so. Jesse would be shot in the back by Bob Ford and Ford would get remembered as "a dirty little coward."

One time Miss Nix had tried to sing "The Ballad of Jesse James" but she forgot how it went. Her memory had played out right where the song says, "And the children they were brave." I took it as far as I could for her, through the verse about Mister Ford. I knew there was a verse about the Glendale train, but before I could sing it I'd lost the words too. But I remember how good it made us feel that morning to sing that song, Miss Nix crooning after me in her rickety high voice, "and laid poor Jesse in his grave." We'd been glad to be alive and singing that morning, no matter what was happening to people anywhere else in the world. This was before the thing came up about John, and before my troubles with the French Canadian caused me to leave town on the run.

I picked up the folder with the rest of the unanswered letters and carried it over to the lake. At first the pages didn't want to go into the water. They kept flapping up in the breeze and flying back against my legs. I kicked them away until they floated out.

For a while I could see some of the pages being pulled along just under the surface of the water. Then there was nothing but ripples. I felt the way people do who like taking out the garbage—glad to make a sign to the past that some of it can be disposed of forever. I understood there were things I wasn't ever going to solve, like the right and wrong of what happened to Miss Nix. And if my own ending fell to her kind of luck, I would just have to hope somebody, even a stranger, would give me help and comfort. But for now, I was ready to take up my life and do the next thing I could.

Beneficiaries

Louise started up the stairs to the Personnel office. On the landing she stopped to look down. It was one of those winding staircases that allowed a panoramic view of the large marble entrance area.

She and Stanley had just moved to this city and had recently accepted employment with the same company. They had been glad to move. They hoped to make a place for themselves so they would not have to move again. The day before, she had filled out forms, signed things, had the ID picture taken. Now it was Stanley's turn.

As she approached the receptionist she heard, from behind the partition, a voice say "beneficiary."

"My children. I want to name my children," she heard Stanley say.

"Do you want the amount shared equally?"

"Equally," Stanley said.

Doors opened and closed in other parts of the building and Louise felt her strength seem to slip downward in her body. But the sensation passed as quickly as it had come and she was able to move toward the stairs. There was a white gloom of light falling from an arch of glass panes above the entranceway, illuminating the marble pattern of the floor. She took her time going down the steps. When she reached the lobby she stood in the core of light and waited for Stanley. She looked up through the cold glaze and saw that it had begun to snow again. The sky seemed to be hurling itself in steady bits of matter at the glass.

He took her arm and guided her outside. The wet flakes collided with her forehead and cheeks, her open eyes. They hurried toward the car. Louise got inside while Stanley used his arm to brush snow from the windshield. Snow continued to fall into the space he cleared, then cleared again. He got in, started the engine and turned on the wipers. The wipers spanked the windshield viciously. Louise was reminded of a symphony conductor she'd seen, maniacally enforcing his little triangle of influence with a baton. When they were into traffic Louise thought she could bring up what had happened.

"I'm sorry I heard it," she said, "but I did. You were naming your children as your beneficiaries."

Stanley took his eyes off the road for a minute and looked at her. "Does that surprise you? Wouldn't you put your children down if you had children?"

"I don't have children," Louise said, "so I can't think of them. I know these things aren't supposed to matter when people love each other. I feel foolish even talking this way, but it made me lonely. Yesterday I named you my beneficiary, then today I had to hear you hadn't even thought of me," she said. Then she said, "It made me feel strange, like something changed when I heard that."

"Because I have children and you don't?" he said.

"Your *children?*" she said. "They're in their twenties. They're adults."

"They're still my children," he said. "And I'm surprised at you. That you'd want to deny them. I'm surprised at you."

They were nearing the mall. Stanley turned his head from side to side as he watched for cars. Then he negotiated the turn into the lot. There were tall gray mounds of snow here and there. He got as close to the entrance of the store complex as he could and parked the car. They had come because they needed to buy curtains for the house, but they did not get out of the car. Louise felt Stanley hadn't understood what had happened to her and she wanted to make him understand, even if she was wrong about it.

"It isn't the money," she said at last. "It's the thought that if you were to die you wouldn't have thought of me, of what would become of me. What if you died and I got sick?" she said.

"But I *do* think of you. Before anyone," he said. "You're always first." He was trying to keep his voice steady but Louise could hear exasperation breaking through.

"Not this time. You were first with me but I wasn't first for you," she said. She hated the sound of her voice saying this. But she didn't stop herself. "I'm just sorry I heard it," she said again.

Their breaths had fogged the windows. The snow falling to the windshield seemed strange and furry.

"If you had children I know you would have done the

same thing," he said. "You wouldn't judge me like this if you had children."

"I'm not judging," she said. "I just feel sad. I can't get out of feeling sad. It isn't your fault. It just hit me. I was standing there like I wasn't there. But I was, and I had to hear you forget me. . . . Maybe I should have named someone else too."

It was cold in the car and now so much snow had fallen onto the windshield that she couldn't tell if it was still falling.

"Maybe you should have. Maybe you should," Stanley said, his voice going up a notch. "I didn't do this to hurt you. You know you're the most important person in my life." He put his arms awkwardly around her shoulders and drew her face to his chest where some snow had melted. "Here, here," he said. She could smell the damp wool of his coat.

"Let's go in," he said, rubbing her back. "Let's buy our curtains and go home and get our house set up." When he opened the door a fringe of snow dropped onto his knees. He got out and stood brushing it off while Louise scooted across the seat and stepped out on his side.

Inside the mall, people still had on their coats. It was a curious inside-outside feeling she was having and it made her want to sit down, but all the benches were taken. It was like a huge, luxurious train station but the trains were all on their way to other cities, so everyone was having to amuse themselves by spending money and waiting for the trains to come back.

Stanley guided her toward an escalator. They rode up on different steps. He looked back at her. Then he reached and took her hand from her pocket and she let him. They rose on the escalator, leaving an entire first-story world behind. They were deposited onto a floor where goods from a gigantic house seemed to have accumulated. There were baby beds, clothes hampers, lamps of every kind, mattresses, coffee tables and window dressings. They passed a counter heaped with pillows. Stanley stopped and began to pinch them and to read their labels aloud.

"We need some good pillows," he said. "Let's get goosedown pillows. Okay? Let's do it." He picked up a pillow by its middle and put his head on it, trying it out as he stood in the aisle. "Hey, feel this," he said, handing the pillow to Louise. It had a plastic covering which was cold to her cheek. But she couldn't get the feel of it because she was standing. She wanted to lie down with it and not have to go any farther. Stanley had walked to the far side of the display. She put the pillow on the floor and lay down in her coat with her purse beside her. As if from far away, she could hear the hum of shoppers.

"This one says 'Goosedown,' but it's the name of the company. That beats all. The pillow is a hundred percent polyester," Stanley's voice carried to her. "You have to watch them every minute," he said.

But Louise had closed her eyes. She lay very still and listened to the sound of feet passing, an overlay of sounds coming to her in little scufflings and shocks to the floor. She did not worry about anyone finding or seeing her. She unbuttoned her coat and pulled her knees up. She lay under the white, fluorescent light and thought of the snow falling over the building, and she thought of the trains moving deeper and deeper into the snowy countryside.

They laughed about it later that night. How she had lain right down in the middle of the department store with her pillow and how she had taken a long while to answer him when he had stood over her.

"I was dreaming," she said.

The house began to get settled, but with both of them working it was hard to keep it as neat as they liked. Stanley suggested they hire a woman to come in once a week and clean, so they did that. At first Louise was too shy with the woman to tell her what she really needed done, but she'd solved this by leaving lists on the kitchen counter. Louise asked her to be sure to dust in the bedroom and this was how the mail she kept near her jewelry box was moved onto the nightstand where Stanley found it.

She was adding to a grocery list from the recipe for a casserole when Stanley came into the kitchen with the letter from Personnel. He handed it to her out of its envelope so she would know he'd seen it.

"Did you do this out of spite?" he said.

She took it from him and put it back into its envelope without looking at it.

"No," she said. "I just felt more—more equal this way."

"That's pretty calculated," he said. "To go back like that and change what you decided before. Who'd you name instead of me? An ex-husband?"

"I'm not trying to be mean," she said. But the minute she said it she thought that maybe she was. Maybe she did want to hurt him. "I've got my brother's children. They've got a long way to go in this world, and if I kick off, well then they'll have some help."

"I wish I hadn't looked at that letter," he said. "I wish I hadn't found out you'd done this. It feels like you're trying to get even or something."

Louise looked down at the photograph of the casserole with all the portions waiting to be divided onto the white plates stacked beside it.

"It makes me feel ugly to talk like this, but it's *my* death and *my* business," she said and shut the book. "I'm supposed to remember you, to think about you, but you don't do the same for me. I've just tried to make things fair again, that's all."

Stanley was leaning against the counter near the door to the basement. He took the lid off an empty mayonnaise jar on the counter and began using it for an ashtray.

"I have to tell you," he said, "it was not your proudest moment when you tried to make me feel like a traitor for naming my own children as my beneficiaries. I wouldn't ever tell that to anyone if I were you. I think you'd come off looking pretty bad."

Louise took a dishrag and began to collect the crumbs off the top of the toaster into her palm. Then she washed her hands under the tap and dried them on her apron. Their breakfast dishes were still in the sink. She took a scrub brush and began to scrub the food from the plates into the disposal. The dishes rattled and clashed against each other.

She turned to him. "If you want people to know, *you* tell them," she said. She felt even if he was right—that everyone would think her unreasonable in this—she would have to be able for that. "How can you decide what my proudest moment is, anyway? You can't decide that. God alone knows that." Even though she'd just mentioned God she felt godless and heartless, as though nothing could soften her again or hold them back from the harm they seemed intent on. What was happening to them was crazy. She didn't know how to be reasonable. They were talking about their deaths, yet they were alive and each of them was sure they were not going to be the one who died first.

What you imagined affected you: Louise could see that now. It did not stay in the mind. It got into the heart and into your words and changed the things you had hoped would give comfort. It stripped you bare, this imagining. It laid you in your grave and counted out your belongings and told you who would weep, who would go through your closets, taking what they needed.

"What can we do?" Stanley asked.

But it seemed to her he already knew there was nothing to be done. He didn't say anything for a minute. He drew on his cigarette.

"I don't know what we can do," she said. "I feel like I've passed right out of the world. Like we're out there on the other side looking back."

"Louise," he said. "Let's stop this." He ground his cigarette out in the mayonnaise lid.

She turned back to the sink. But she could feel him behind her, and then she felt the pressure of his hands at her waist. She held her palms steady under the flow from the tap. She felt the flesh on her arms ripple. He leaned against her so she felt her pelvic bones push against the counter. His lips touched the nape of her neck. He pushed harder. The warm water kept running.

Bad Company

M<small>RS</small>. H<small>ERBERT</small> <small>DROVE INTO THE CEMETERY</small>, parked near the mausoleum, and got out with her flowers. The next day was Memorial Day, and the cemetery would be thronged with people. Entire families would arrive to bring flowers to the graves of their loved ones. Tiny American flags would decorate the graves of the veterans. But today the cemetery was still and deserted.

When she reached her husband's grave she saw that someone had been there before her. The little metal vase affixed to the headstone was crammed with daffodils and dandelions. Whoever had put them there hadn't known the difference between a flower and a weed. She set her flowers down on the flat gravestone and stared at the unsightly wad of flowers. Only a man could have thrown together such a bouquet, she thought.

She raised her hand to her brow and looked around. A short distance away she saw a girl stretched out next to a grave. She hadn't seen her at first because the girl had not been standing. The girl lay propped on one elbow so she could look down at the gravestone next to her. When Mrs. Herbert walked toward her, the girl did not lift her head or move. Then she saw the girl pluck a blade of grass and touch it to her lips before letting it fall. Mrs. Herbert's shadow fell across the girl, and the girl looked up.

"Did you happen to see anyone at that grave over yonder?" Mrs. Herbert asked.

The girl raised herself into a sitting position. She looked at the woman, but didn't say anything.

She's crazy, Mrs. Herbert thought, or else she can't talk. She regretted having spoken to the girl at all. Then the girl stood up and touched her hands together.

"There was a man. About an hour ago," the girl said. "He could of been to that grave."

"It's my husband," Mrs. Herbert said. "His grave. But I don't know who could have left those flowers." She noticed that the grave next to the girl had no flowers. She wondered at this, that anyone would come to a grave and then leave nothing behind. At this time of day the shadows of the evergreens at the near end of the graveyard crept gradually across the grass. It sent a chill through her shoulders. She drew her sweater together at the neck and folded her arms.

"He didn't stay long," the girl volunteered. And then she smiled.

Mrs. Herbert thought it was a nice thing after all to speak to this stranger and to be answered courteously in this sorrowful place.

"He was over at the mausoleum too," the girl said.

Mrs. Herbert thought hard who it might be. She only knew one person buried in the mausoleum. He had been dead ten years now and only one member of his family still survived. "It must have been Lloyd Medly," she said. "His brother, Homer, is over there in the mausoleum. His ashes, anyway. They grew up with my husband and me, those boys." She had spoken to Lloyd just last week on the telephone. He was in the habit of calling up every few weeks to see how she was. "Homer's on my mind a lot," he'd said to her when they last talked.

"I don't know anybody in the mausoleum," the girl said.

Mrs. Herbert looked down and saw a little white cross engraved over the name on the stone. There were some military designations she didn't understand and, below the name, the dates 1914–1967. "Nineteen-fourteen! That's the year I was born," she said, as if surprised that anyone born in that year had already passed on. For a moment it seemed as if she and the one lying there in the ground had briefly touched lives.

"I can barely remember him," the girl said. "But when I stay here awhile, things come back to me." She was a pretty girl with high Indian cheekbones. Mrs. Herbert noticed the way her hips went straight down from her waist. She had slow, black eyes, and appeared to be in her late twenties.

"I can't remember what Homer looked like," Mrs. Herbert said. "But he could yodel like nobody's business. Yodeling had just come in." She thought of Lloyd and how he said he and Arby, another brother, had been lucky to get out of California alive after they'd gone there to bring Homer's body back. Homer had been found dead in a fleabag hotel with Lloyd's phone number in his shirt pocket. "They'd as soon knock you in the head in them places as to look at you," Lloyd said afterwards.

"He was a street wino," she said to the girl. "But he was a beautiful yodeler. And he could play the guitar too."

"I think my dad used to whistle," the girl said. "I think I remember him whistling." She gazed toward the grove of trees, then across the street to the elementary school building. No one was coming in or going out of the building. It occurred to Mrs. Herbert that she had been to the cemetery hundreds of times and had never once seen any children coming or going from the school. But she knew they did, as surely as she knew that the people buried under the ground had once walked the earth, eaten meals, and answered to their names. She knew this as surely as she knew Homer Medly had been a beautiful yodeler.

"If I died tomorrow, I wonder what my little girls would remember," the girl said suddenly. Mrs. Herbert didn't know what to say to this so she didn't say anything. After a moment the girl said, "I'd like to start bringing my girls with me out here, but I hate to see kids run over the graves."

"I know what you mean," Mrs. Herbert said. But then she thought of her own father. Something he had said when he'd refused to be buried in the big county cemetery back home in Arkansas. "I want to be close enough to home that my grandkids can trample on my grave if they want to." But, as it turned out, everyone had moved away, and it hadn't mattered where he was buried.

"I always try to walk at the foot of the graves," the girl said. "But sometimes I forget." She put her hands into the hip pockets of her jeans and looked toward the mausoleum. "Those ones that are ashes, they don't have to worry," she said. She took her hands out of her pockets and sat down again on the grass next to the grave. "Nobody walks over them," she said. "I guess they just sit forever in those little cups."

Mrs. Herbert considered the idea of Homer's remains being contained in a little cup. She was glad she'd never have to see it. Then she remembered that Lloyd had said he and his brother had wanted to bring Homer's body back, but there was too much red tape. And then there was the expense. So they'd had him cremated and, between them, they'd taken turns on the train holding the box with his ashes in it until they got home. Remembering this made her want to say a few words about Homer. She'd met Homer in her girlhood at nearly the same time she'd met her husband. For a moment, the thought came to her that Homer could have been her husband. But just as quickly she dismissed the thought. What had happened to Homer had made a deep, unsettling impression on her. She and Lloyd had talked about it once when they'd spoken in the supermarket. Lloyd had shaken his head and said, "Homer could of been something. He just fell in with the wrong company." And then he hadn't said anything else.

The girl brushed at something on the headstone. "My father was killed in an accident," she said. "We'd all been in swimming and then we kids went to the cabin to nap. My mother woke us up, crying. 'Your daddy's drowned,' she said. This drunk tried to swim the river and when my father tried to save him, the man pulled him down. 'Your daddy's drowned,' she kept saying. But you don't understand things when you're a kid," the girl said. "And you don't understand things later either."

Mrs. Herbert was struck by this. She touched her teeth against her bottom lip, then ran her tongue over the lip. She didn't know what to say, so she said: "There's Homer that lived through the Second World War and then died in California a pure alcoholic." She shook her head. She didn't understand any of it.

The girl stretched out on the ground once more and made herself comfortable. She looked up and nodded once. Mrs. Herbert felt the girl slipping into a reverie, into a place she couldn't follow, and she wanted to say something to hold her back. But all she could think of was Homer Medly. She couldn't feature why she couldn't get Homer off her mind. She wanted to tell the girl everything that was important to know about Homer Medly. How he had fallen into bad company in the person of Lester Yates, a boy who had molested a young girl and been sent to the penitentiary. How Beulah Looney had gone to the horse races in Santa Rosa, California, in 1935, and brought back word that Homer was married, and to a fine-looking woman! But the woman didn't live very long with Homer. He got drunk and hammered out the headlights of their car, then threatened to bite off her nose.

But she didn't tell the girl any of this. She couldn't. Besides, the girl looked to be half asleep. Mrs. Herbert thought it seemed the most natural thing in the world for the girl to be lying there alongside her father's grave. Then the girl raised up on one elbow.

"I came out here the day of my divorce," the girl said. "And then I kept coming out here. One time I lay down and fell asleep," she said. "The caretaker came over and asked me was I all right. Sure, I said. I'm all right." The girl laughed softly and tossed her black hair over her shoulder. "Fact is, I don't know if I was all right. I been coming here trying to figure things out. If my dad was alive I'd ask him what was going to become of me and my girls. There's another man ready to step in and take up where my husband left off. But even if a man runs out on you it's no comfort just to pick up with the next one that comes around. I got to do better," the girl said. "I got to think of my girls, but I got to think of me too."

Mrs. Herbert felt she'd listened in on something important, and she wished she knew what to say to the girl for comfort. She and her husband hadn't been able to have children and, like so much of her life, she'd reconciled herself to it and never looked back. But now she could imagine having a daughter to talk with and to advise. Someone she could help in a difficult time. She felt she'd missed something precious and that she had nothing to offer the girl except to stand there and listen. Since her husband's death nearly a year ago it seemed that she seldom did more than exchange a few words with people. And here she was telling a stranger about Homer and listening to the girl tell her things back. Her memory of Homer seemed to insist on being told, and though she didn't understand why this should be, she didn't want this meeting to end until she'd said what she had to say.

The shadows from the stand of trees had darkened the portion of the cemetery that lay in front of the school building. The girl tilted her head toward the place her father was lying, and Mrs. Herbert thought she might be praying—or about to pray.

"Well, I've got peonies to put out," Mrs. Herbert said, and she moved back a few steps. But the girl did not acknowledge her leaving. Mrs. Herbert waited a minute, then turned and headed back across the graves. The ground felt softer than it had when she'd approached the girl, and she couldn't help thinking each time she put her foot down that she had stepped on someone.

She felt relieved when she reached her husband's grave. She stood on the grave as if there at least she had a right to do as she pleased. The grave was like a green island in the midst of other green islands. Then she heard a car start up. She turned to look for the girl, but the girl was no longer there. The girl was gone. Just then Mrs. Herbert saw a little red car head out of the cemetery.

She took hold of her flowers and began to fit them into a vase next to the flowers she guessed must be from Lloyd. Once, a few weeks earlier, Lloyd had stopped at her house on the way to the cemetery and she'd given him some flowers to take to Homer and some for her husband.

"They were roarers, those two," Lloyd had said as she'd made up the two bouquets. She thought of her husband again. He'd been a drinker like Homer and, except for having married her, he might have fallen in with bad company and ended the way Homer had.

She took her watering can and walked toward the spigot that stood near the mausoleum. She bent down and ran water into the can as she rested her eyes on the mausoleum. Bad company, she thought. And it occurred to her that her husband had been *her* bad company for all those years. And when he hadn't been bad company, he'd been no company at all. She listened to water run into the metal can and wondered what had saved her from being pulled down by the likes of such a man, even as Lester Yates had pulled Homer Medly down.

She let herself recall the time her husband had flown into a rage after a drinking bout and accused her of sleeping around, even though every night of their married life she'd slept nowhere but in the same bed with him. He'd taken her set of china cups out onto the sidewalk and smashed them with the whole neighborhood looking on. From then on they'd passed their evenings in silence. She would knit and he would look after the fire and smoke cigarettes. God knows it wasn't the way she'd wanted things. She'd thought she'd done the best she could. But the memory of those long, silent evenings struck at her heart now, and she wished she could go back to that time and speak to her husband. She knew there were old couples who lived differently, couples who took walks together or played checkers or cards in the evenings. And then it came to her, the thought that she had been bad company to him, had even denied him her company, going and coming from the house with barely a nod in his direction, putting his meals on the table out of duty alone, keeping house like a jailer. The idea startled and pained her, especially when she remembered how his illness had come on him until, in the last months, he was docile and then finally helpless near the end. What had she given him? What had she done for him? She could answer only that she had been there—like an implement, a shovel or a hoe. A lifetime of robbery! she thought. Then she understood that it was herself she had robbed as much as her husband. And there was no way now to get back their life together.

The water was running over the sides of the can, and she turned off the spigot. She picked up the watering can and stood next to the mausoleum and stared at it as if someone had suddenly thrown an obstacle in her pathway. She couldn't understand why anyone would want to be put into such a place when they died. The front was faced with rough stones and one wall was mostly glass so that visitors could peer inside. She had tried the door to this place once, but it was locked. She supposed the relatives had keys, or else they were let in by the caretaker. Homer was situated along the wall on the outside of the mausoleum. Thinking of Homer made her glad her husband hadn't ended up on the wall of the mausoleum as a pile of ashes. There was that to be thankful for.

When she reached his grave she poured water into the vase and then stared at the bronze nameplate where enough space had been left for her own name and dates.

She remembered the day she and her husband had quarreled about where to buy their burial plots. Her husband had said he wasn't about to be buried anyplace that was likely to cave into the ocean. There were two cemeteries in their town—this one just off the main highway near the elementary school, and the other which was located at the edge of a cliff overlooking the ocean. He did not want to be near the ocean. He had said this several times. Then he had gone down and purchased two plots side by side across from the school and close to the mausoleum. She hadn't said much. Then he had shown her the papers with the location of the graves marked with little *X*'s on a map of the cemetery. The more she thought about it, though, the more she set her mind on buying her own plot in the cemetery overlooking the ocean. Then one day she arranged to go there, and she paid for a gravesite that very day.

She hadn't meant to tell her husband about her purchase, but one night they'd quarreled bitterly, and she'd flung the news at him. She had *two* gravesites, she said— one with him and one away from him; and she would do as she pleased when the time came. "Take your old bones and throw them in the ocean for all I care," he told her.

They'd left it like that. Right up until he died, her husband hadn't known where his wife was going to be buried. But what a thing to have done to him! To have denied him even that small comfort. She realized now that if anyone had told her about a woman who had done such a thing to a dying husband she would have been shocked and ashamed for her. But this was the story of herself she was considering, and she was the one who'd sent her life's company lonely to the grave. This thought was so painful to her she felt her body go rigid—as if some force had struck her from the outside, and she had to brace herself to bear it.

She'd taken comfort in the idea of the second grave, even when she couldn't make up her mind where she would finally lie. She had prolonged her decision and she saw this clearly now for what it was, a way to deny this man with whom she had spent her life. Even when she came to the cemetery where her husband lay, she would still be thinking, as she was now, about the cemetery near the ocean—how when she went there she could gaze out at the little fishing boats on the water or listen to the gulls as they wheeled over the bluff. An oil tanker or a freighter might appear and slide serenely across the horizon. She loved how slowly the ships passed, and how she could follow them with her eyes until they were lost in the distance.

She gave the watering can a shake. There was water left in it, and she raised the can to her lips and drank deeply and thought again of the ocean. What she also loved about that view was the thought that those who walked in a cemetery, any cemetery, ought to be able to forget the dead for a moment and gaze out at something larger than themselves. Something mysterious. The ocean tantalized her even as she felt a kind of foreboding when she looked on it with her own death in mind. She could imagine children galloping over the graves, then coming to a stop at the sharp cliff edge to stare down at the waves far below. Her visits to the cemetery near the ocean gave her pleasure even after her grave there was no longer a secret. When her husband asked, "Have you been out there?" she knew what he meant. "I have," she said. And that was the extent of it. She thought she understood those who committed adultery and then returned home —unfaithful and divided. Yet she did nothing to change the situation. Then he had died, and some of the pleasure in her visits to the other grave seemed to have gone with him. As Mrs. Herbert's life alone had settled into its own routine, weeks might go by until, with a start, she would realize she hadn't been to either cemetery. The fact of her two graves became a mystery to her.

The shadows of the evergreens had reached where she was standing. She saw that the school building across the street was entirely in shadow now. She gathered up the containers she'd used to carry flowers to the grave and picked up her garden shears. On her way to the car she turned and looked at the flowers on her husband's grave. They seemed to accuse her of some neglect, some false-hood. She had decorated his grave, but there was no com-fort in it for her. No comfort, she thought, and she knew she had simply been dutiful toward her husband in death as she had been in life. The thought quickened her step away from there. She reached her car and got in. For a moment she could not think where it was she was supposed to go next.

A month passed after her visit to the cemetery. Daisies and carnations were in bloom, but Mrs. Herbert made no visit to her husband's grave. It was early on a Sunday when she finally decided to go again. She expected the cemetery to be empty at that time of the morning, but no sooner had she arrived than a little red car drove into the narrow roadway through the cemetery and parked near the mausoleum. Then the driver got out. Mrs. Herbert was not surprised to see that it was the young woman she'd met before Memorial Day. She felt glad when the girl raised her hand in greeting as she passed on her way to her father's grave.

The girl stood by the grave with her head down, thinking. She had on a short red coat and a dress this time, like she might be on her way to church. Mrs. Herbert approved of this—that the girl was dressed up and that she might go on to church. This caused another kind of respect to come into the visit. But what she felt most of all was that this was a wonderful coincidence. She had met the girl twice now in the cemetery and she wondered at this. Mrs. Herbert thought it must mean something, but she couldn't think what.

Mrs. Herbert took the dead flowers from the vases and emptied the acrid water. There was a stench as if the water itself had a body that could decay and rot. She remembered a time in her girlhood when she and Homer and her husband had been driving to a dance in the next county. The car radiator had boiled over and they'd walked to a farm and asked for water. The farmer had given them some in a big glass jug. "It's fine for your car, but I wouldn't drink it," the man said. But the day was hot and after they'd filled the radiator each of them lifted the jug and took a drink. The water tasted like something had died in it. "Jesus save me from water like that!" Homer had said. "They invented whiskey to cover up water like that." Her husband agreed that the water tasted bad, but he took another drink anyway.

Mrs. Herbert straightened and glanced again toward the girl. She seemed deep in thought as she stood beside the grave. Mrs. Herbert saw that once again the girl had brought no flowers with her.

"Would you like some flowers for your grave?" Mrs. Herbert called to her. The girl looked startled, as if the idea had never occurred to her. She waited a moment. Then she smiled and nodded. Mrs. Herbert busied herself choosing flowers from her own bunch to make a modest bouquet. Then she stepped carefully over the graves toward the girl. The girl took the flowers and pressed them to her face to smell them, as if these were the first flowers she'd held in a long time.

"I love carnations," she said. Then, before Mrs. Herbert could stop her, the girl began to dig a hole with her fingers at the side of her father's headstone.

"Wait! Just a minute." Mrs. Herbert said. "I'll find something." She walked to her car and found a jar in the trunk. She returned with this and the girl walked with her toward the mausoleum to draw water to fill the container. The water spigot was near the corner of the mausoleum where Homer's ashes lay, and she remembered having told the girl about his death.

"There's Homer," Mrs. Herbert said, and pointed to the wall of the mausoleum. There were four nameplates to each marble block, and near each name a small fluted vase was attached to the stone. Most of the vases had faded plastic flowers in them, but Homer's vase was empty. The girl opened and closed her black eyes, then lifted her flowers and poured a little of the fresh water into the container fastened to Homer's stone. Then she took two carnations and fitted them into the vase. It was the right thing to do and Mrs. Herbert felt as if she'd done it herself.

As they walked back toward the graves Mrs. Herbert had the impulse to tell the girl about her gravesite near the ocean. But before she could say anything, the girl said, "I've got what I came for. I been coming here asking what I'm supposed to do with my life. Well, I'm not for sale. That's what he let me know. I'm free now and I'm going to stay free," the girl said. Mrs. Herbert heard the word "free" as if from a great distance. *Free*, she thought, but the word was meaningless to her. It came to her that in all her visits to her husband's grave she'd gotten nothing she needed. She'd just as well go and stand in her own backyard for all she got here. But she didn't let on to the girl she was feeling any of this, and when they set the container of carnations on the grave she said only, "That's better, isn't it."

"Yes," the girl said. "Yes, it is." She seemed then to want to be alone, so Mrs. Herbert made her way back to her husband's grave. But after a few minutes she saw that instead of staying around to enjoy the flowers, the girl was leaving. She waved and Mrs. Herbert thought, *I'll never see her again*. Before she could bring herself to lift her hand to wave goodbye, the girl got into her car. Then the motor started, and she watched the car drive out of the cemetery.

A week later the widow drove to the cemetery again. She looked around as she got out of the car, half expecting to see the little red car drive up and the girl get out. But she knew this wouldn't happen. At her husband's grave she cleared away the dead flowers from her last visit.

She had brought no flowers and didn't quite know

what to do with herself. She looked past the mausoleum and saw that a new field was being cleared to make room for additional graves at the far end of the cemetery. The sight brought a feeling of such desolation that she shuddered. She felt more alone than she had ever felt in her life. For the first time she realized she would continue on this way to the end. Her whole body took on the dull hopelessness of the feeling. She felt that if she had to speak she would have no voice. She was glad the girl wasn't there, that she would not have to speak to anyone in this place of regret and loneliness. Suddenly the caretaker came out of a shed in the trees, turned on a sprinkler and disappeared back into the shed. Then, once again, there was no one.

She waited a minute, and then lowered herself onto the grave. The water from the sprinkler whirled and looped over the graves, but it did not reach as far as her husband's grave. She looked around her, but saw no one. She leaned back on the grave and stretched out her legs. She put her head on the ground and closed her eyes. The sun was warm on her face and arms and she began to feel drowsy.

As she lay there she thought she heard children running and laughing somewhere in the cemetery. But she couldn't separate this sound from the sound of the water, and she did not open her eyes to see if there really were children. The sprinkler made a *whit-whit* noise like a scythe going through a field of tall grass.

"I'm going to rest here a moment," she said out loud without opening her eyes. Then she said, "I've decided. You bought a place for me here, and that's what you wanted. And that's what I want too."

She opened her eyes then and with an awful certainty she knew that her husband had heard nothing of what she had said. And not in all of time would he hear her. She'd cut herself off from him as someone too good, someone too proud to do anything but injury to the likes of him. And this was her reward, that it would not matter to anyone on the face of the earth what she did. This, she thought, was eternity—to be left so utterly alone and to know that even her choice to be buried next to him would never reach her husband. Was she any better than the meanest wino who died in some fleabag hotel and was eventually reduced to ashes? No, she understood, no better. She had been no better than her husband all those years, and if she had saved him from a death like Homer's, it was only to die disowned at her own hearth. The enormity of this settled on her as she struggled to raise herself up.

A light mist from the sprinkler touched her face, and when she looked around her, she saw a vastness like that of the ocean. Headstones marked off the grass as far as she could see. She saw plainly a silent and fixed company set out there, a company she had not chosen.

She looked and saw the caretaker in the doorway of the shed. He drew on his cigarette as he stood watching her. She raised her hand and then brought it down to let him know she had seen him. He inclined his head and went on smoking.

The Wimp

THE DAY MY BROTHER, GORDON, kicked me out of his house and called me a bitch I wanted my husband to let go like Rocky Marciano. But Mel's not like that. All he did was to take my arm, the way he used to when he was teaching me to bowl, and say to my brother, "That's enough, Gordon." Then he walked me to the car. He was trembling. Sure, I was trembling, too. But I was furious. I was mad at them both.

When Gordon opened the door that afternoon of the day I'm talking about, his face changed. "Where's Momma?" he said. Mel wanted to shake hands with Gordon, but Gordon just clapped him on the shoulder so Mel had to drop his hand. "Vina's in the kitchen," Gordon said. Mel put his hand into his pocket, and we went on into the house.

Gordon had expected our mother to be there, and, according to him, we should have brought her. After all, it was her grandson's birthday, wasn't it? It didn't matter to him that she was in her eighties and maybe didn't feel like spending the time she had left with a brat kid. Who would? I didn't say this though. All I said was "Momma's getting up in age, Gordon." He looked at me like he wanted to take a bite out of me. Anything I said would have been wrong. He and our mother had been on the outs because of a chainsaw. Gordon had borrowed it from her, then given it back with the chain broken. She'd said something to Gordon to the effect that his father would turn over in his grave if he knew a son of his had treated his chainsaw that way. Then Gordon told her where to get off. "It's just one of those things that happen in families," Mel had said at the time. But I'd known then that neither Gordon nor my mother was about to forget it. I went ahead and took off my coat.

Dinner was on the table, and Vina said for everyone to sit down. So we sat down on benches at either side of the table. We settled ourselves and began to pass things when Gordon did something that beat anything. He took a couple of bites of bean salad, then dropped his fork in his plate and stood up.

"I don't have any appetite," he said. "I've lost my appetite. Anyway, I've got things to do." He moved over and put his big hands on his son's shoulders. George had a turkey-frank in both hands and was biting it into chunks and then spitting them back onto his plate.

"Eat up, Kid," my brother said, leaning down close to him. "We got a birthday to celebrate, and tomorrow we're going fishing, right?"

"No fireworks," Vina put in, "unless you eat that up."

George crammed more turkey-frank into his mouth, stared at Gordon and started to chew.

Gordon is a tall, rangy guy, a nervous guy—what I call "cold nervous." He must've gotten that way when he worked as a cop and had to control his temper. He says things in a calm, reasonable voice, but the rest of him is jumping. I could see his arm muscles flexing and tensing below his T-shirt sleeves as he headed for the basement door.

"I'll have some of that chicken, please, Vina," Mel said.

Vina tried to act like this sort of thing always happened when she had people over for dinner. She lit a cigarette and smoked while she cut up the rest of the turkey-frank on George's plate. Every now and then Vina took a puff from her cigarette, then took a bite of food from George's plate. George began reciting what each of the fireworks could do until Vina told him to shush up and eat.

"Gordon always saves some fireworks from the Fourth to shoot off on Kid's birthday," Vina said, then plumped a big dollop of potato salad onto my plate. George jumped up and grabbed something off the kitchen counter. He stuck it right under my nose. It was cone-shaped and wrapped in soft transparent tissue paper with illustrations of castles and dragons.

"It sprays colors around and around. Then it falls into the lake," George said. "This one makes a big boom, then a big bunch of white shoots out. Then it falls into the lake." Before he could go on, we heard an awful banging and clattering coming from the basement. I took another helping of beans and tried to catch Mel's eye. He was scratching at his shirt collar and staring out over the lake at some water-skiers. All at once Gordon let go with a string of curses. Then we heard a noise like something had been thrown down hard on the floor. It was quiet for a minute. Then the noise started again. I saw Vina light another cigarette. I heard a scraping noise close by, looked over, and saw it was Mel. He was running his knife back and forth across his plate. I lifted the plate out from under his knife and set it down next to mine. He just raised his eyebrows and folded his hands on the table.

"Gordon's working on his outboard motor," Vina said finally. "He's down there hours at a time. Last night he was at it until nearly midnight." Everything is always just fine with Vina. Just fine. Even when all hell is breaking loose. Drives me nuts. "How about some cake? Let's have some birthday cake pretty soon, okay?" she said. Gordon kept banging away down below us.

"I want fireworks," George said. He flung himself onto the carpet yelling, "Boom-boom, boom-boom!" Then he ran to the counter again and held up a wide belt of firecrackers. "These just go pop-pop, pop-pop-pop," George said. "They're not pretty. They just scare you, and you have to watch your fingers. They might blow your fingers off."

Just at that minute some women and children wandered into the kitchen while we were going at the last of the food. They hadn't knocked, or if they had, I hadn't heard, with all the other commotion. There were three mothers and several kids.

"Hey, you guys!" Vina said. "Just in time for birthday cake." She got up and started to punch candles into a chocolate cake on the counter. Mel was watching Vina's cigarette, afraid some ash was going to drop onto the icing. He got up and handed her a paper plate.

Twilight had come down over the lake. One of the mothers brought out some sparklers. They looked like miniature cattails until they were lit. Then suddenly they began to glow and dart. They made a white electric light and a hissing noise as the children galloped the length of the deck, scribbling in the air with them. I felt a moment of weakness for kids—everybody's kids.

"Let's get out of here," I whispered to Mel.

"What about the cake?" he said.

"Forget about cake," I said. "Let's go." We got up and I took our plates to the counter, where Vina was setting out paper plates for the cake. As quick as we got up, there were kids in our places at the table.

"We have to be going, Vina," I said.

"Before cake?" Vina said. "Mel, you want some cake, don't you?" She stood there with a knife in her hand, ready to cut the cake. But I thought she was going to cry. Mel looked at the cake and then at me. He put on his cap and shrugged. He didn't say anything though. Vina went over to the basement door and opened it. "Honey! Gordon! Come up here, honey. Your sister's leaving and they haven't even had any cake." Then she turned and said, "I just can't believe you're leaving." She lit another cigarette. We heard Gordon making his way up the stairs. When he came into the room he looked at me hard.

"Leaving already," he said. "I'll bet you're heading straight over to Momma's. Je-sus," he said. "This is enough to drive a man crazy twice. Well you tell her what she missed, okay?" His arm muscles bunched as he looked at Vina. Vina looked scared. She took a breath and held it. "Don't you *ever* put me through anything like this again," Gordon said to Vina. "Inviting people over here, then letting them leave." Vina put down the cake knife and ran some water over her cigarette. Then Gordon swung around to Mel and me. "What was the reason you said Momma didn't come to our party?"

"I told you Momma was tired," I said. "She's just tired out."

"Well goddamn her anyway," Gordon said. Mel and I were inching toward the door. "You tell her that if she can't make it to her own grandson's birthday party I've got no goddamn use for her."

I looked and saw the mothers of the other children listening to what was happening. They couldn't figure out what was going on any more than I could. Vina was holding a stack of cone-shaped party hats. She handed a hat to one boy, and he stood there holding it. Mel took his cap off and wiped his head and then put it back on again. I saw Vina had begun to cry onto her arm, still holding the party hats. I was mad as a hornet to hear Gordon talk like this about our mother in front of a room-ful of kids and strangers. It was then I said exactly what I thought.

"I don't carry those kind of messages to my mother. You tell her yourself, if that's the kind of man you are." Then Gordon was right in my face.

"Bitch!" he said. "You're just like her." Then the clincher came. The moment when Mel should have decked him.

"Get the hell out of my house, bitch," Gordon said. "And don't you ever set foot in here again." His jaw mus-cles were working all the way down into his neck. Then Mel said, "That's enough, Gordon," and walked with me out to the car.

I was boiling. I was on the moon I was so mad. I gave Mel an earful all the way home. He clenched his teeth on his pipe and let me tear away.

"What the hell was I supposed to do?" he asked, after a while. "Get my head knocked off? An old, nearly retired guy like myself hit a strapping guy like that? You got to be nuts."

"You could have said something. Let him know you were on my side anyhow." I'd never been kicked out of anyplace. I felt humiliated. "You should have told him he can't talk like that to his sister," I said. But it was a lost cause. It also hit me that I had no place to kick anybody out of myself, assuming I ever wanted to kick anybody out. The company Mel sold house trailers for had given us one to live in, but we didn't own anything resembling a home.

Mel turned the radio on to a music station that was playing old pop tunes. He set his pipe deeper into his mouth and kept driving. I guess he thought it would simply all blow over.

The next morning I woke up still sizzling.

"What's eating you?" Mel said, after I'd burned the toast and made the coffee too strong to drink.

I didn't answer right away. I'd decided that instead of tearing into Mel again I'd better go into town. "I got things to do," I said after a while. There was some smoked fish from Mel's fishing trip the week before that I wanted to mail out to friends and some other errands that needed doing.

A fat woman was ahead of me in line at the post office. She had two little rat-faced kids hanging onto her. She was holding a package that was wrapped and taped every which way.

"Do you know the zip code for Kodiak, Alaska?" she asked me.

"I don't," I said.

"I knit my husband some socks and I'm sending them to him while I got the money," she said. "He went up there to work in the woods, logging. But he got laid off. They kick them out of the woods when it gets too hot."

The next thing I knew, I was telling this blubbery woman things best kept to myself.

"My brother kicked me out of his house the other day," I said. "And if that wasn't bad enough, my husband just stood there like a dumb cluck and didn't say diddly." There I was standing in line at the post office and telling her this stuff. "It hurts a woman's pride," I said. "Whatever happened to men who defended your honor?" I was out of breath, so I shut up, and besides, I saw that other people in line had turned to stare at me.

"My husband's a wimp too," this fat woman said, and

then she took her fat hand and patted my arm with it. "You got to grin and bear it," she said, looking down at her two rat-faced kids like they were all anybody could expect for the offspring of a wimp. I hadn't come into a public place to be told that my husband was a wimp. Then her turn came and she moved up to the counter.

That night Mel and I started on a new puzzle. It was a Japanese garden with a little bridge, some stunted trees and huge gray boulders. I watched Mel sorting through the pieces with the tip of one finger. *Wimp*, I thought. She called him a wimp. Then something occurred to me. Maybe he is a wimp, I thought. Still, I felt like a traitor, and when Mel asked me later did I want to play a few hands of casino, I said no, I was tired. But really it was because there were things I needed to sleep on.

"I'm tired too," he said. Mel checked to see that the doors were locked, and we got ready for bed. After he'd climbed in, he said, "You okay?"

"I'm fine," I said. "Fine."

The next day Mel wanted to drive into town to get a haircut.

"What's there to cut?" I said. I always said this when Mel said he was going to get a haircut. It was a joke, but now I looked at the strip of hair along Mel's neck and it looked silly, it really did, and this time I meant it when I wondered what they were going to cut.

"Drives me nuts to have hair in a place I want kept nice and shiny," Mel said. I said I'd ride along and pick up a few mason jars.

"If you don't find me at the barbershop, I'll be in the sporting goods store," Mel said.

At the supermarket I found the canning supplies I wanted. But there were no wide-mouthed lids. I signaled a clerk, a heavily made-up woman in her late fifties, and asked her if they had more lids in stock.

"Everybody's canning," she said. "I've stocked this section three times today."

"I'm making peach preserves," I said. Then it happened again. Things came out of my mouth I hadn't the least intention of saying. "I usually make some preserves for me and my husband," I said. "Then I make extra for my brother's family. But my brother kicked me out of his house the other day and called me a bitch. And if that wasn't enough, that husband of mine just sat there like a toad on a log. That's the last preserves of mine that bunch will eat."

The woman gave me a look, as if what I'd said was about to set her off. But then a sweet expression came over her face.

"That brother of yours," she said. "He ought to be ashamed. And that husband too. If I'd been there I'd of said worse than *bitch* back to him. I'd given them both something to remember!" she said.

I hadn't gone into the store for sympathy, but it wasn't so bad to be offered a little. Still, I hadn't asked this old cartoon of a woman to volunteer an opinion. Or maybe I had. She held up some lids.

"No, no," I said. "Wide-mouthed lids! I need wide-mouthed lids." Then it hit me that I had better do something about the fact that I couldn't keep my mouth shut about the incident with my brother. I felt scared of myself, like maybe Gordon wasn't the only crazy one in our family. I got out of there with the jars as quick as I could.

Out on the sidewalk I thought, Maybe I'm getting to be like those batty old women who jabber on street corners. Maybe someday I'll just stand around yelling to whoever walks by that my husband kicked me out, or I kicked him out, or God knows what.

At the barber's there was a man in the chair and a man waiting, and neither of them was Mel. The barber, a young guy wearing a striped tie, was running the clippers up the back of the neck of the man in the chair. The radio was on and the clippers were making a mean electric sound inside the music.

"I'm looking for my husband," I said when the barber glanced up. He shut off his clippers and stepped over the little piles of hair as he came toward me.

"Who?" he said. "What's his name?"

"My husband," I said.

"A little guy just left," the barber said and snapped his clippers back on. "Little balding guy."

"He's not so little," I said, "and he's not so bald." I heard the clippers snap off, and then the gulf opened again and I felt as if I'd cast off into a large body of water without an oar or a sail. What's happening to me? I thought. "He's not a wimp, if that's what you mean," I shouted at the barber. He took a step back from me into the hair. I saw that the customer who was waiting had put down his paper, and the man in the barber's chair had managed to swivel himself toward me.

"Look, I just cut hair," the barber said.

"My husband may be bald and short," I said. "Okay. But he's not the kind who stands by." Then I heard myself take everything a step further. "Just the other day," I said, "he kicked my brother out of our house for his foul-mouthed insults." Now I'd done it. I'd plunged into the deep, and the things I was saying bore no resemblance to the truth.

"Lady, do you want a haircut?" the barber said, like he was talking to a six-year-old. "I cut hair. That's *all* I do here."

It was then I noticed that the barber himself was the next thing to bald. A strange feeling of power and freedom came over me. I looked at myself in the wide horizontal mirrors that ran the length of the barbershop. I had a nice head of hair and I seemed a little taller than I'd remembered. I turned my back and strode out of the shop.

The sporting goods store was just a few doors down the street. When I walked in, I spotted Mel on the other side of the store. He was over near the tents and sleeping bags. Then he moved a few steps and began to flex the tip of a fishing rod. He's a short bald man who likes to go fishing and to put puzzles together, and he sells trailer houses. If Gordon were to walk in here right now, Mel would probably say, "Hello Gordon, how's it going?"

I was glad to see my husband, but for a minute I didn't let him know I was there. I just watched. It was nice seeing how he enjoyed that fishing rod. What could he do against a maniac like my brother Gordon anyway? My being a woman was probably all that had kept Gordon from slamming me a good one. And even that wasn't much of a deterrent. Then it struck me that if Mel hadn't been with me, I might be walking around with a few less teeth or maybe I wouldn't even be walking around.

I stood in the sporting goods store next to the hip boots and canteens and wondered at the codes between men over when to fight and when to cut losses and run, or just walk off like Mel had. Words came easy to me, but I'd never had to break a knuckle on anybody over principles or insults. I watched Mel pretend he was casting with the fishing rod, testing the weight and movement of the pole. He had an exact feel for it. I could see that. He knew just what he was doing with that rod.

I had my canning jars and Mel had his haircut. We were going back to the trailer, and I was going to make some peach preserves. Mel put the fishing rod in its rack again, rubbed his hand across the bald dome of his head and looked up and saw me. He waited a minute and looked back at the rod. Then he was smiling and walking in my direction.

No, I thought, he's not a man who'd sweep anyone away. But I felt light-headed, and something of what I'd felt earlier at the barbershop seemed to leap up in me when I looked at his kind face. He caught hold of my arm and walked me toward the glass doors. He pressed one of the doors open with his shoulder and held it, until he had seen me through. He took my arm again and we went on like that down the sidewalk so that people made way for us, or sometimes we made way for them and smiled as if we knew them. We passed the movie house and a furniture store, then a bar where a man had just careened from the doorway.

"I'm not begging yet," the man said, as we tried to step around him. "If I ask you for money I'm not begging," he said. "You got something for me?" he said. "I'm asking, just asking." He was drunk, but he seemed angry. He was right in our faces now, and I smelled the liquor.

Mel let go of my arm and reached into his pocket. He took out a crumpled bill. It could have been a hundred-dollar bill for all he cared. He just wanted to go on down the sidewalk to the car. He was even willing to pay to get there. As we stepped away from the man, Mel lifted his chest and a sigh came out of him like a stab of pain that passed into me. I understood then that the dangers of manhood were all around us. And I felt I knew intimately what he was thinking and feeling, this peaceable good man I had meant to squander with blows against my brother.

Desperate Measures

TERENCE MCBRIDE CUT A TRENCH right down through the middle of our lives. May Cunningham was the first to say so. But she was also the one who cared the least for him when he went to work with us that summer at our town newspaper.

Because May was a woman, the idea persisted that she had more patience than anyone else at the *Herald* and was, therefore, better at teaching the temporary help. She *was* a good teacher; they had that right. But not because of her patience. May Cunningham simply hated to see anything done badly, and she went over and over a thing until you were numb from it, could do it by rote, thought you had been born into the world for that purpose alone.

Such an apprenticeship generated enough tension that anyone could have seen Terry McBride didn't have a fool's chance of succeeding with May Cunningham. For Terry took no time at all in letting us know that he had his own way of doing things, even things he didn't know how to do.

He would listen to May's painstaking instructions, nodding and keeping his own counsel. Then he would go off, and do the task in some unthinkable other way. It did not help matters that he did things well. This fact was to make our memory of him all the more baffling as we tried later to figure out who this man was, and why he had come into our midst only to be carried beyond our small-town lives by an event none of us could comprehend at the time, nor even to this day.

I was seventeen years old when this was happening. It was the second summer I'd had this job on the paper. I was beginning to live and sleep the rhythms of my town through the gossip and facts I sifted daily in the newsroom conversations. That spring I had been kissed two or three times by a boy I cared nothing about whose main recommendation was a knack for algebra. Before that summer was out, his passion would escalate to fever pitch while I tried to figure out how to tell him I was sorry, but I wasn't the girl for him, and besides, that I knew my future was someplace else, though I didn't know where.

It was true I had more direction than most girls of our town. I wanted to go to college, though I had no idea what I would study or how I would support myself. I still lived at home with my brothers and parents. Each day I would look at them as if a reprieve had been granted and I was being allowed to fix their faces in memory once and for all before setting out on a long journey.

To such a girl, Terry McBride was an emissary of near-Promethean proportions. When he walked into a room, all my attention and sympathies were drawn out of me toward whatever he was saying or doing. He was in his mid-thirties and handsome in a lean, direct way. He had let it be known that his presence among us was due to some temporary shift in his fortunes; that he was used to far more exciting enterprises than took place in our barren quarters, where staff members worked stolidly at typewriters around one long, scarred wooden table.

Terry let it slip to May that he had been a stock car racer. By the time he got around to telling me, I had already taken a deep draught of May's outspoken conviction that Terry McBride was a liar and a braggart. But it made no difference. I believed him with a silent fervor, though I had never seen a stock car race, and thought of it as something men did when they wanted to improve their chances of dying early. Nor did I lose allegiance when Packy Thompson, the wire editor, told us at lunch, with obvious disdain, that McBride "claimed" to have been a bush pilot in Alaska.

"He couldn't fly his own spit to my shoe," Packy said, and tossed Jimmy Deets, the sports editor, a candy bar from his lunch bucket.

My own status on the staff was somewhere between that of a mascot and an industrious robot who had attained the requisite capacities of hearing, sight, speech and mobility. Everyone was fond of me, and as a sign of this, an occasional plum in the way of jobs was tossed offhandedly in my direction, as when I was allowed to call the police department to get the report of traffic tickets, or told to phone the Coast Guard station for the weather report.

The rest of the time I rewrote publicity announcements prepared by various clubs and organizations in the town, or spooled the yellow Associated Press wire tape for the linotype machine. I attached each section to its appropriate teletyped copy with a clothespin, and arranged them on Packy's desk so he could select the news he would run for the day. It was a job, and I felt lucky to have it, instead of selling ice cream or cleaning fish at the local cannery.

Terry McBride did not ask me if I was dissatisfied. He simply began to speak in my behalf each time he saw a chance.

"Let the kid do that," he'd say when something worthwhile came up, as if it were an obvious idea. The upshot of such suggestions was that a day came when I was actually given an assignment which took me out of the office. Terry, whose main responsibilities were as darkroom technician and photographer, was to go with me. He couldn't have been happier.

"What about them ducks!" he said to me as we climbed into Marie, the cranky Oldsmobile that served as the staff car. He said this a lot when things got interesting.

"She reminds me of a sweetheart I had in Key West in the fifties," Terry said. "You had to choke her to get her started."

He knew this wasn't the kind of thing you said to a young girl, but it seemed he couldn't help himself. I was sure what he'd said had something to do with sex. But then much of what Terry said was in this vein, and if a person decided to be offended they would have a full-time job for themselves.

"I can't listen to any more of his vulgar stories," May Cunningham would complain to Packy. "He's trying to ruffle me. He wants to keep me torn up. If you ask me, he's a bona fide kook."

But that day, Terry and I had escaped the confines of the newsroom and the orders of its harried crew. I remember thinking of the office as if it were a ship afloat among the imaginings and doings of the town and of the world. Cryptic messages trailed in its wake: "Russians Eye West Coast Fish"; "Attraction of Communism Emotional, Not Intellectual"; "Woman Slaps Bear—Bruin Slaps Her Back."

Terry and I had begun to keep a list of such favorites on the back of an old copy sheet in the lunchroom. To this we added headlines we made up to suit our whimsy and, as Terry put it, "to get poetry back into the life of the guy on the street." The best of the season had come a few days before. I'd found it scrawled in huge block letters on a piece of photo paper on the ledge I called my desk. NO DEATH DELAY FOR HEMINGWAY, it read. And Terry was likely, after that, to chant this with a jazzy beat when he wanted to liven things up, which was often.

But the day of our assignment, Terry said something about Hemingway which made me hear his jingle in a new register.

"I read everything the guy wrote," he said. "He wasn't just cleaning his gun and then shot himself in the head by accident. No sir. Papa had it down. When the jig's up, it's up."

Hemingway had been found dead from a gunshot wound on July 3, and his wife had made up a statement for the press which was read by a friend—what Terry called a "pack of damned lies." He lowered his head and quoted the sentence that now finished all his references to Hemingway, a line from Gary Cooper's widow. "They're in the barn now," he said, as he pulled to a stop at the address we'd been given. "Papa's in the barn."

He set the hand brake and we got out and went around to the backyard of the two-story brick house. A doctor's family lived there and the doctor's eight-year-old son was reported to have built a magnificent tree house. Or at least this is what the doctor had leaked to the press—the press in this case being Packy, the doctor's fishing partner. We had been given the tongue-in-cheek assignment to "bring back the goods on this tree house."

We wouldn't have cared if we had been sent out to the County Fair to photograph blue ribbons on hogs. We felt almost glamorous to be "out on assignment." In the best tradition of investigative journalism, we began to consider, as we looked up at the tree, the serious implications our article might have on the prospects of tree houses of the future in our town and possibly the world. For, to Terry's way of thinking, at any moment one might, by some act of daring, turn the key in the door to one's fortunes, for better or worse. This belief, like all his stratagems for life, was not something he talked about. It was implicit, I knew even then, in the pleasure he took and excited in others as he approached even the humblest task.

That day spent in the tree house with Terry now seems engraved in my record book of perfect days. It was a day of lightning and silver, like treasure stolen from an unsuspecting ship on the high sea. A day in which we moved through the world in a calm radiance, far from the grapplings and stirrings of the young mistaken love of the algebra wizard.

"Well kid, where do you want me?" Terry said after we'd brought the doctor's son out and photographed him with the tree house from every conceivable angle. "You're the boss," Terry said.

I led him up the rope ladder to photograph a tree-house view of the neighborhood and then to get some shots of the interior. The tree house was cozy, fitted out like a miniature house with a rug and scraps of mismatched wallpaper. There were other amenities, such as bookcases and a cardboard box marked ICE CHEST, inside of which we found a milk carton labeled TOP SECRET. We opened it and found it full of rocks, shells and tattered insects wrapped in cellophane. Terry sat back on his heels under the low ceiling through which eyelets of tree and sky were visible.

"I could live here," he said. "This is all a man needs. By God, this is all right." He cranked the arm of the Rolleiflex and then focused on the doctor's son, who was standing like an exile at the foot of the tree looking up. Terry snapped the picture, then glanced around the miniature room looking for his next target.

He picked up a comic book from the bookcase and then tossed it back on the shelf. "Crap," he said. "A doctor's son and he reads crap." It was as if some misconception about the advantages of the privileged had suddenly been laid to rest.

"This place could use some imagination," he said, after a moment. "If it were mine, I'd run a waterproof tower made out of a couple of shower curtains right up around this trunk all the way to the top. Then I'd mount a telescope on a revolving pedestal where the tree crowns. A person could take in the constellations. Count meteors. Think about the universe and what the hell this is all about. This boy hasn't begun to make use of this tree."

Then Terry leaned out the hole that served as a window and called down to the boy. "Come on up here, son. Is this any way to treat guests?" He took his camera from around his neck and settled back against the wall. I hunched my knees under my chin and folded shut my notebook. Soon the boy's serious face peered from under the door flap.

"How about some hospitality," Terry challenged. "I'll have a whiskey with a beer on the side, and my companion will take a gin and tonic with a twist of lime, if you don't mind."

The boy stared at us as if we'd been deposited there by interplanetary forces, and now he would just have to make the best of it. He crawled to a shelf and took down two plastic glasses. Then he reached to the back of the ice chest and brought out a bottle of Coke, which he opened with a section of his intricate pocketknife. He handed us our drinks, then crouched on his knees, holding the bottle, in which a little Coke remained.

"Let me propose a toast," Terry said, raising his glass.

"To the world of tree houses. To the lasting and the ever-lasting. And to things just for this day."

This is eloquence, I thought; this is style. Our glasses met, as the boy, in a trance of submission, extended his arm, to which a Coke bottle had somehow become af-fixed.

Terry, as it developed, had performed magic tricks somewhere back in the ever-widening gulf of his past. And now he took out a pack of cards and began to shuffle them accordion-like back and forth in the air. Before long, the day began to move into that intimate time which belongs to childhood, and to things we treasure and ulti-mately leave behind as having no currency in the unmys-terious business of our daily lives.

For a while that day, my relentless course toward adulthood was suspended. I could forget that the algebra wizard had hinted significantly that he might be loaned his father's mammoth Buick for the weekend. For now, there was only this makeshift house infused with birdsong and the reprieve of closeness with Terry and the young boy, our accomplice. We plunged into the blue afterglow of dusk, until someone came out of the distant and insig-nificant shelter of the house below, and called his name as if he were lost or had thoughtlessly abandoned them.

After that Packy saw to it that Terry and I kept to the office. It may also have been his idea that Terry should train me for the darkroom. If his intent was to make Terry insecure about his job, to make him feel that even a kid could do it, the ploy was a failure. With enthusiasm, the magician, stock car racer and bush pilot began to initiate me into the skills and rituals of developing and printing film. In the dim glow of the red printing light we arranged supplies, adjusted the hypo bath and developing fluid. Then darkness. Our bodies side by side in the narrow confines of the room. Looking back, it seems strange that nothing untoward took place, for Terry let it be known that he had an eye for the ladies.

"I've thrown better-looking ones than that out of bed," he said one day as we printed the languid face of some newly engaged high school graduate. He sloshed her image around in the chemicals, then submerged the photograph in the clear tap water and snapped on the light.

His shirt sleeves were rolled up to the elbow, and it was then I saw the bolt of a scar across the underside of his wrist. He caught my glance and said in a matter-of-fact voice, "A jaguar slashed me there." I looked at him and realized for the first time he was lying; and that he saw I knew this.

He said no more and we stumbled into the daylight as if darkness had spewed us out new-made and molten in our separate and unknown identities. Still, it was as if a gentle circle of agreement began immediately to form around us, protecting the as yet undecided consequences of what had happened between us.

The world news had taken on a new intensity, of which we were dimly aware. Eichmann was standing trial in Jerusalem and several columns a day on the front page were given over to the account. The first American airplane had been hijacked to Cuba. President Kennedy was beefing up the military, trying to head off the establishment of the Berlin Wall. He had called on the reserves and asked that draft boards double or triple the number of young men to be drafted.

But in our town the news remained essentially unspectacular. A bridge spanning the canal and costing twenty-seven million dollars (it would eventually collapse in a windstorm) had just been dedicated and opened. There had been a spaghetti-eating contest at one of the churches, which Terry had photographed. All eating instruments, including hands, had been forbidden, and even the mayor had participated. Three men had been caught after they had stolen twelve gallons of wine and two cartons of cigarettes from a small grocery.

None of these events chastened or enriched our lives to any significant degree. At best they helped to assure the townspeople that the world was a more or less fair and decent place. That justice could be had, even though any number of young men in uniform in readiness in America could not prevent the Berlin Wall.

The occurrences that were to wrest Terry McBride from our midst are inextricably linked in my memory to matters over which I had no control, such as the possibility of war breaking out over Berlin. In an article entitled "Sees Chance of War" a general had answered "No" when asked as to whether a Berlin War would be likely to turn into a nuclear war. But as I read the piece fresh off the teletype that morning before anyone else had arrived for work, I wondered what such a question could mean. And whether I should be afraid. And what, if anything, I could do.

It did not help matters that Terry McBride arrived that morning dressed peculiarly in calk boots, a pair of patched dungarees, a logger's plaid shirt and suspenders, and a fishing hat studded with hand-tied flies.

"Are you going out for the logrolling contest?" I asked when he failed to greet me. He was pacing back and forth before the manager's cubicle just off the newsroom. Suddenly the phone rang. When I answered it a woman's voice asked for Terry. He came in and picked up a phone at the other end of the news table and began to reassure, or console, and then to plead with the woman.

"Okay, honey. Okay, baby," he said and then he hung up, took off his cap and struck it against one of the typewriters hard. "Damn," he said. Then he walked a few paces with the hat in his hand, turned back and slapped it down on the typewriter again.

He put the hat back on over his crew cut and leaned

forward, both hands gripping the table, his head down as if containing some energy he didn't yet know what to do with. My stomach had begun to feel queasy. I stopped winding the wire tape and wondered for the second time that morning what to do.

"Is something wrong?" I ventured.

"You could say so," Terry said. "Yes, 'wrong' is a fair assessment."

"Tell me what it is," I said and went partway around to his end of the table. Terry began to pace again and to glance anxiously toward the main door as if he was afraid someone might come in on us. Then gradually he began to talk as a man talks when he is desperate and talk is all he has.

"I went in yesterday and asked for a raise and they turned me down," he said. "There's just no way I can make it. I'm in debt and I can't figure it anymore." Then he paused and stared at the table where, in an hour, all the staff members would be hurrying toward their deadlines.

"Terry," I said, "I've got a little money saved. I've got three hundred dollars. If you need it, you can have it."

He looked up as if he were seeing me for the first time that morning. His face seemed blanched of emotion.

Suddenly he stepped over behind one of the support pillars near the passageway to the darkroom. I could still see his shoulders and hear a muffled sound. I had never seen a man cry. But Terry was somewhere beyond shame and pride, and at last he moved into view and turned toward me.

"I can't take your money, little lady," he said in a voice still only partially composed. "But I'll tell you this, if I'd ever had a daughter, or a sister, I would have wanted her to be just like you."

These were the last words of any import that Terence McBride was to say to me. He sat down at Packy's typewriter then, as if my offer to give him my savings had freed him toward what he had to do. He typed a brief note, drew it out of the typewriter, and handed it to me.

"Tell him I'll be down at the coffee shop if he wants to talk to me," he said. Then he pulled on the brim of his hat and walked out the door into the rest of his life.

The note was his resignation, and when Packy came in I gave it to him. I told him Terry was down at the coffee shop if he wanted to talk to him.

"What's to say?" Packy said. He shrugged and tossed the note down on the news desk. Packy did not go down to the coffee shop. By the time my break came and I went down, Terry McBride was gone.

A little over two weeks passed after Terry quit his job. It was August and hot. Packy had just ordered a banner for the front page which read "President Sounds Berlin Warning." The telephone rang and I remember Packy's voice veering up as he told whoever it was to hold it; then he got a pencil and began to scratch on his pad the information the voice on the phone was giving him. When he hung up he sat a moment as if considering how he should feel. Then he stood and adjusted his trousers on his hips.

"Terry McBride has robbed the Forks bank of forty-six thousand dollars," Packy said. He grabbed his hat and looped a camera around his neck. "He's down at the jail," he said, looking back at us with a strange, rueful smile on his face.

After Packy had left, May Cunningham motioned me over to her desk and told me to sit down in the chair alongside her. Jimmy Deets came around to sit on the table. The others stopped work to see what May was going to tell. Only Hank Morris, the oldest man on the staff, who typed with the index finger of each hand, continued to work.

"About a week before Terry quit work," May said in a confidential tone, "my husband and I were down to the Kiwanis Club for an evening. Who do you think was the entertainment? Well I thought this had to be a joke. Terry McBride came out and sat down at the piano. He sat there a minute and then he started to play. He played the smoothest Eddie Duchin jazz you'd ever want to hear."

May was telling us this as if it had bearing on the news we were all still struggling to believe—that Terry McBride was a bank robber.

"I changed my opinion about Terry the minute I heard him play that jazz," May said. "There's something to him after all, that's what I thought. But now I don't know what to think."

When Packy came back he acted like he was too busy to tell us anything at first. Then he stopped rushing in and out of the room, and began to talk his notes to us, as if we were the surviving, but disinherited, relatives of the man whose actions he was presenting.

Packy could not sit still. He stood up at his end of the table as if a man had to stand to tell such a story. He said that the day Terry had quit the paper he'd gone out to Forks, a town three hours away from our town, near the place where he'd grown up.

"He knew that area like the palm of his hand," Packy said. "He was born at Clearwater."

Then Packy said that Terry had tried to find a job, but nobody would hire him. All he had was a rusted-out .22 rifle. He headed into the woods with that to try to live off the land.

Game was scarce and he couldn't catch any fish, Packy said. But finally, after three snaps of the hammer, he got a shot off, and brought down a grouse. He cooked it and ate it. That grouse was about the only substantial food he'd eaten during the two weeks he spent in the woods.

Then Terry went into town, into Forks, and began to walk the streets, fingering the last coin he had in his pocket.

At this point May's phone rang, and Packy paused in his story. May said a few quiet words and hung up.

Packy flipped a page in his notes and went on. According to the way Terry told it, he had this one nickel left so he decided to flip it. If it came up heads, he would rob the bank. And if it came up tails he would shoot himself. The coin came up heads.

"But did he say *why* he did it when you saw him?" Jimmy Deets asked Packy.

"Nope," Packy said. "He just shrugged. Said he didn't know."

"You know what Willie Sutton said when they asked him why he robbed banks?" Jimmy said. "He said, 'That's where the money is!' " Everyone laughed nervously at this, but we were all waiting to hear the rest of what had happened to Terry.

Packy went on. Terry had gone into a grocery store and asked for two paper sacks. Then he wrapped the rifle in a pair of old denims. Once inside the bank, Terry had leaned on the rail and talked to a teller he knew, Ella Paulson, until the bank closed. Then he'd simply gone over to a teller he didn't know, and handed her a set of detailed instructions. But it turned out she was a slow reader and Terry got impatient. "This is a holdup," he yelled, and unwrapped the gun. He herded the bank employees into the vault, where he told them to stay until four o'clock.

There were money sacks in the vault and they were stuffed with fat packages of bills, mostly in fives, tens and twenties, and there was $10,000 in fifties. A photograph of the money would appear in our paper the next day with the caption "Loot" and, standing next to it, with big smiles on their faces, the local sheriff's men.

But in Packy's story, Terry still had the loot and was busy taking his first hostage, Gerald Morhead, the bank manager. He told Morhead that he was holding his kids. No one would find them for months unless the banker did just as he was told. Then he gave Morhead the job of chauffeuring his first bank robber out of town. In the bank manager's Volkswagen, they headed north on the highway, back toward our town.

We listened to Packy tell how, as Terry neared the Lawson ranger station, he pulled over and made Morhead take off his shoes and socks. Then he put the man out by the side of the road and, driving with the bank manager's empty shoes next to him, he continued to make his way on the one road out of there around the lake. Meanwhile Morhead hobbled barefoot to the ranger station and called home to make sure his kids were safe. Then he alerted the sheriff and gave them his license plate number and a description of his car.

Next came the roadblocks. As I listened, I thought of the morning Terry had left and how he had refused the meager savings I'd offered. How, even as he'd driven his stolen getaway car, he had no idea that he had just pulled the biggest bank robbery in the history of the state.

"Well, it's the stupidest thing I ever heard of," May said. "Anyone would know you couldn't get away coming around that lake. He should have headed for the woods."

"Sounds like he'd had enough of the woods," Jimmy said. "Sounds like he was scared as hell."

Packy said that maybe if Terry hadn't gotten boxed into traffic behind a broken-down logging truck he might have made it as far as the ferry docks. But he never would have made it into Canada. They would have stopped him.

One thing was clear, and that was that we'd all wanted Terry to get away, and for a few minutes during Packy's account, we had thought like bank robbers—had driven with a man's empty shoes riding next to us and stacks of money in the backseat.

"Stan Nymen from our bank is over at the station counting the money right now," Packy said. "He thinks it's all there, but they're counting it anyway." He took a roll of exposed film out of his pocket and tossed it to me. "It's all yours, kid. Get in there and do your stuff."

When Terry had quit, I had been pressed into service in the darkroom. It was a kind of promotion. But today's job was one I could have done without. I stood in the newsroom and dreaded the dark and the photographs of my friend as if I had been sent to the morgue to identify a body.

Packy flipped through his notes hurriedly to see if he had missed anything.

"Just a minute, gang," he said. "Here's the clincher. Terry had a record. He was on probation for impersonating a park official."

Everyone began to laugh. Everyone except me. Finally the laughter died down, and May remembered what she thought was a significant clue to Terry's character.

"He was always telling me the plot of some spy thriller or detective story," she said. "Sometimes he'd read all night, he told me. Well, it didn't make him any smarter, did it?" she said, as if that put the cap on Terry McBride —stock car racer, bush pilot, jazz musician, entertainer of children and fighter of jaguars. I thought of telling them that Terry was also a reader of Hemingway, but decided against it.

I put on Terry's apron and went into the darkroom. There I labored like an embalmer the rest of the morning in the acrid stench of chemicals. One after the other, the negatives flashed into the brief light of the enlarger, and I saw the face of the captive seep onto the photographic paper again and again. He had the look of a deer caught in someone's headlights in the middle of the road. His wrists were handcuffed together. Behind him I saw the bars of his cell as he walked from it toward the elbow of someone just out of the picture. He looked thinner, but he was clean shaven and his crew cut seemed to have been freshly trimmed. I'll go and see him, I thought. And then I began to cry, because I knew that I would not go, and that I would never see Terry McBride again.

Packy gave the robbery a banner that day across the top of the front page. It had none of the classic import of headlines I remembered from a scrapbook my grandmother had kept on the Dalton brothers' attempt in 1892 to rob two banks at once in Coffeyville, Kansas, their hometown. The outlaws had been gunned down and their corpses heaped in the street. "A Remarkable Occurrence," "A Most Terrific Battle," "A Desperate Attempt," and "Literally Wiped Out," the headlines had read. But the photographs of Terry appeared with the caption "Confessed Robber" and the banner said only "Forks Bank Robber Apprehended."

"He wanted to get caught," May said, as we all stared at the first copy of the paper, fresh from the presses. "Any fool could have pulled a better robbery than that."

Her remarks seemed designed to push what had happened into the past before Terry had been sentenced. And soon enough the news of the world crowded out the news of the robbery. The banner headline the following day read "Berlin Situation May Be Longstanding."

Terry McBride was bound over to Federal officials and eventually sentenced to twenty-five years at the McNeil Island Prison. Only once after he left our town did we have word of him, and that was some months later. An article appeared on the wire service about a daring escape, the first ever made from the McNeil Island Prison. The escapee had managed to swim to the mainland, where, for an entire day, he hid in his wet clothes. The sheriff had found Terry McBride not far from shore—as May described it, "huddled in some bushes."

But in those long hot summer days we did not know of Terry's brief escape. He was simply Terry-the-liar-and-impersonator, Terry-the-failed-bank-robber. But I remembered one perfect day of beauty and eloquence and time at a standstill, though I never spoke of it. I think I was perhaps the only one on the paper who didn't surrender to May's ideas that all Terry McBride wanted was to be back in prison where he could play piano and entertain the other prisoners.

But what did I know? I was only a young woman of mostly good intentions who was about to break the heart of a young man by telling him the truth. That I didn't love him. And that I hoped never again to be wrestled out of my clothes in the back seat of a car in the blasphemous name of love.

Girls

ADA HAD INVITED HERSELF ALONG on the four-hour drive to
Corvallis with her daughter, Billie, for one reason: she
intended to see if her girlhood friend, Esther Cox, was still
living. When Billie had let drop she was going to Corval-
lis, Ada had decided. "I'm coming too," she said. Billie
frowned, but she didn't say no.

"Should I wear my red coat or my black coat?" she'd
asked Billie. "Why don't I pack a few sandwiches." Billie
had told her to wear the red coat and said not to bother
about sandwiches; she didn't like to eat and drive. Ada
packed sandwiches anyway.

Billie had on the leather gloves she used when she
drove her Mercedes. When she wasn't smoking cigarettes,

she was fiddling with the radio, trying to find a station. Finally, she settled on some flute music. This sounded fine to Ada. "Keep it there, honey," she said.

"Esther was like a sister to me, an older sister," Ada said. "I don't know anyone I was closer to. We did the cooking and housekeeping for two cousins who owned mansions next door to one another—the Conants was their name. Esther and I saw each other every day. We even spent our evenings together. It was like that for nearly four years." Ada leaned back in her seat and stole a look at the speedometer: 75 miles an hour.

"It's like a soap opera," Billie said. "I can't keep the names straight or who did what when." She brought her eyes up to the rearview mirror as if she were afraid someone was going to overtake her.

Ada wished she could make her stories interesting for Billie and make it clear who the people were and how they had fit into her life. But it was a big effort and sometimes it drove her to silence. "Never mind," she'd say. "Those people are dead and gone. I don't know why I brought them up." But Esther was different. Esther was important.

Billie pushed in the lighter and took a cigarette from the pack on the dash. "What are you going to talk to this person about after all these years?" she said.

Ada considered this for a minute. "One thing I want to know is what happened to Florita White and Georgie Ganz," Ada said. "They worked up the street from us and they were from Mansfield, where Esther and I were from. We were all farm girls trying to make a go of it in the city." Ada remembered a story about Florita. Florita, who was unmarried, had been living with a man, something just not done in those days. When she washed and dried her panties she said she always put a towel over them on the line so Basil, her man, couldn't see them. But that was all Ada could remember Florita saying. There had to be more to the story, but Ada couldn't remember. She was glad she hadn't said anything to Billie.

"You might just end up staring at each other," Billie said.

"Don't you worry," Ada said. "We'll have plenty to say." That was the trouble with Billie, Ada thought. Since she'd gone into business, if you weren't *talking* business you weren't talking. Billie owned thirty llamas—ugly creatures, Ada thought. She could smell the llama wool Billie had brought along in the back seat for the demonstration she planned to give. Ada had already heard Billie's spiel on llamas. There were a lot of advantages to llamas, according to Billie. For one thing, llamas always did their job in the same place. For another, someone wanting to go into the back country could break a llama in two hours to lead and carry a load. Ada was half inclined to think Billie cared more about llamas than she did about people. But then Billie had never gotten much out of people, and she *had* made it on llamas.

"Esther worked like a mule to raise three children," Ada said.

"Why are you telling me about this woman?" Billie said, as if she'd suddenly been accused of something. She lit another cigarette and turned on her signal light. Then she moved over into the passing lane. The car sped effortlessly down the freeway.

Ada straightened herself in the seat and took out a handkerchief to fan the smoke away from her face. What could she say? That she had never had a friend like Esther in all the years since? Billie would say something like: *If she was so important then why haven't you seen her in forty-three years?* That was true enough, too; Ada couldn't explain it. She tried to stop the conversation right where it was.

"Anyway, I doubt if she's still living," Ada said, trying to sound unconcerned. But even as she said this Ada wanted more than ever to find Esther Cox alive. How had they lost track? She'd last heard from Esther after Ada's youngest son had been killed in a car crash, twenty years ago. Twenty years. Then she thought of one more thing about Esther, and she said it.

"The last time I saw Esther she made fudge for me," Ada said. "You'll see, Billie. She'll whip up a batch this time too. She always made good fudge." She caught Billie looking at her, maybe wondering for a moment who her mother had been and what fudge had to do with anything. But Ada didn't care. She was remembering how she and Esther had bobbed each other's hair one night, and then gone to the town square to stroll and admire themselves in the store windows.

In the hotel room, Ada hunted up the phone book.

"Mother, take off your coat and stay awhile," Billie said as she sat down in a chair and put her feet up on the bed.

Ada was going through the *C*'s, her heart rushing with hope and dread as she skimmed the columns of names. "She's here! My God, Esther's in the book." She got up and then sat back down on the bed. "Esther. She's in the book!"

"Why don't you call her and get it over with," Billie said. She was flossing her teeth, still wearing her gloves.

"You dial it," Ada said. "I'm shaking too much."

Billie dropped the floss into a waste basket and pulled off her gloves. Then she took Ada's place on the bed next to the phone and dialed the number her mother read to her. Someone answered and Billie asked to speak to Esther Cox. Ada braced herself. Maybe Esther was dead after all. She kept her eyes on Billie's face, looking for signs. Finally Billie began to speak into the phone. "Esther? Esther Cox?" she said. "There's someone here who wants to talk to you." Billie handed Ada the phone and Ada sat on the bed next to her daughter.

"Honey?" Ada said. "Esther? This is Ada Gilman."

"Do I know you?" said the voice on the other end of the line.

Ada was stunned for a moment. It *had* been a very long time, yes. Ada's children were grown. Her husband was dead. Her hair had turned white. "We used to work in Springfield, Missouri, when we were girls," Ada said. "I came to see you after my first baby was born, in 1943." She waited a moment and when Esther still did not say anything, Ada felt a stab of panic. "Is this Esther Cox?" she asked.

"Yes it is," the voice said. Then it said, "Why don't you come over, why don't you? I'm sorry I can't remember you right off. Maybe if I saw you."

"I'll be right over, honey," Ada said. But as she gave the phone to Billie she felt her excitement swerving toward disappointment. There had been no warm welcome —no recognition, really, at all. Ada felt as if something had been stolen from her. She listened dully as Billie took down directions to Esther's house. When Billie hung up, Ada made a show of good spirits.

"I'll help you carry things in from the car," she said. She could see Billie wasn't happy about having to drive her anywhere just yet. After all, they'd just gotten out of the car.

Billie shook her head. She was checking her schedule with one hand and reaching for her cigarettes with the other. "We don't have much time. We'll have to go right now."

The street they turned onto had campers parked in the front yards, and boats on trailers were drawn up beside the carports. Dogs began to bark and pull on their chains as they drove down the street.

"Chartreuse. What kind of a color is that to paint a house?" Billie said. They pulled up in front of the house and she turned off the ignition. They didn't say anything for a minute. Then Billie said, "Maybe I should wait in the car."

The house had a dirty canvas over the garage opening, and an accumulation of junk reached from the porch onto the lawn. There were sheets instead of curtains hung across some of the windows. A pickup truck sat in the driveway with its rear axles on blocks. Esther's picture window looked out onto this. Ada stared at the house, wondering what had brought her friend to such a desperate-looking place.

"She'll want to see how you turned out," Ada told Billie. "You can't stay in the car." She was nearly floored by Billie's suggestion. She was trying to keep up her good spirits, but she was shocked and afraid of what she might find inside.

They walked up to the front door. Ada rang the bell and, in a minute, when no one answered, she rang the bell again. Then the door opened and an old, small woman wearing pink slacks and a green sweater looked out.

"I was lying down, girls. Come in, come in," the woman said. Despite the woman's age and appearance, Ada knew it was Esther. She wanted to hug her, but she didn't know if she should. Esther had barely looked at her when she let them in. This was an awful situation, Ada thought. To have come this far and then to be greeted as if she were just anyone. As if she were a stranger.

A rust-colored couch faced the picture window. Esther sat down on it and patted the place beside her. "Sit down here and tell me where I knew you," she said. "Who did you say you were again?"

"God, woman, don't you know me?" Ada said, bending down and taking Esther's hand in hers. She was standing in front of the couch. "I can't believe it. Esther, it's me. It's Ada." She held her face before the woman and waited. Why wouldn't Esther embrace her? Why was she just sitting there? Esther simply stared at her.

"Kid, I wished I did, but I just don't remember you," Esther said. "I don't have a glimmer." She looked down, seemingly ashamed and bewildered by some failure she couldn't account for.

Billie hovered near the door as if she might have to leave for the car at any moment. Ada dropped the woman's hand and sat down next to her on the couch. She felt as if she had tumbled over a cliff and that there was nothing left now but to fall. How could she have been so insignificant as to have been forgotten? she wondered. She was angry and hurt and she wished Billie *had* stayed in the car and not been witness to this humiliation.

"I had a stroke," Esther said and looked at Ada. There was such apology in her voice that Ada immediately felt ashamed of herself for her thoughts. "It happened better than a year ago," she said. Then she said, "I don't know everything, but I still know a lot." She laughed, as if she'd had to laugh at herself often lately. There was an awkward silence as Ada tried to take this in. Strokes happened often enough at their age so she shouldn't be surprised at this turn of events. Still, it was something she hadn't considered; she felt better and worse at the same time.

"Is this your girl? Sit down, honey," Esther said and indicated a chair by the window stacked with magazines and newspapers. "Push that stuff onto the floor and sit down."

"This is my baby," Ada said, trying to show some enthusiasm. "This is Billie."

Billie let loose a tight smile in Esther's direction and cleared a place to sit. Then she took off her gloves and put them on the window sill next to a candle holder. She crossed her legs, lit a cigarette and gazed out the window in the direction of her Mercedes. "We can't stay too long," she said.

"Billie's giving a talk on business," Ada explained, leaving out just what kind of business it was. "She was coming to Corvallis, so I rode along. I wanted to see you."

"I raise llamas," Billie said, and turned back into the room to see what effect this would have.

"That's nice. That's real nice," Esther said. But Ada doubted she knew a llama from a goat.

"Now don't tell me you can't remember the Conants—those cousins in Springfield we worked for," Ada said.

"Oh, I surely do remember them," Esther said. She was wearing glasses that she held to her face by tilting her head up. From time to time she pushed the bridge of the glasses with her finger. "I've still got a letter in my scrapbook. A recommendation from Mrs. Conant."

"Then you must remember Coley Starber and how we loaned him Mrs. Leslie Conant's sterling silver," Ada said, her hopes rising, as if she'd located the scent and now meant to follow it until she discovered herself lodged in Esther's mind. Billie had picked up a magazine and was leafing through it. From time to time she pursed her lips and let out a stream of smoke.

"Coley," Esther said and stared a moment. "Oh, yes, I remember when he gave the silver back. I counted it to see if it was all there. But, honey, I don't remember you." She shook her head helplessly. "I'm sorry. No telling what else I've forgot."

Ada wondered how it could be that she was missing in Esther's memory when Coley Starber, someone incidental to their lives, had been remembered. It didn't seem fair.

"Mom said you were going to make some fudge," Billie said, holding the magazine under the long ash of her cigarette. "Mom's got a sweet tooth."

"Use that candle holder," Esther told Billie, and Billie flicked the ash into the frosted candle holder.

Ada glared at Billie. She shouldn't have mentioned the fudge. Esther was looking at Ada with a bemused, interested air. "I told Billie how we used to make fudge every chance we got," Ada said.

"And what did we do with all this fudge?" Esther asked.

"We ate it," Ada said.

"We ate it!" Esther said and clapped her hands together. "We *ate* all the fudge." Esther repeated the words to Billie as if she were letting her in on a secret. But Billie was staring at Esther's ankles. Ada looked down and saw that Esther was in her stocking feet, and that the legs themselves were swollen and painful-looking where the pantleg had worked up while Esther sat on the couch.

"What's making you swell up like that?" Billie said. Ada knew Billie was capable of saying anything, but she never thought she'd hear her say a thing like this. Such behavior was the result of business, she felt sure.

"I had an operation," Esther said, as if Billie hadn't said anything at all out of line. Esther glanced toward a doorway that led to the back of the house. Then she raised up her sweater and pulled down the waistband of her slacks to show a long violet-looking scar which ran vertically up her abdomen. "I healed good though, didn't I?" she said. Esther lowered her sweater, then clasped her hands in her lap.

Before Ada had time to take this in, she heard a thumping sound from the hallway. A man appeared in the doorway of the living room. His legs bowed at an odd angle and he used a cane. The longer Ada looked at him, the more things she found wrong. One of his eyes seemed fixed on something not in this room, or in any other for that matter. He took a few more steps and extended his hand. Ada reached out to him. The man's hand didn't have much squeeze to it. Billie stood up and inclined her head. She was holding her cigarette in front of her with one hand and had picked up her purse with the other so as not to have to shake hands. Ada didn't blame her. The man was a fright.

"I'm Jason," the man said. "I've had two operations on my legs, so I'm not able to get around very easy. Sit down," he said to Billie. Jason leaned forward against his cane and braced himself. She saw that Jason's interest had settled on Billie. Good, Ada thought. Billie considered herself a woman of the world. Surely she could handle this.

Ada turned to Esther, and began to inquire after each of her other children, while she searched for a way to bring things back to that time in Springfield. Esther asked Ada to hand down a photograph album from a shelf behind the couch, and they began to go over the pictures.

"This arthritis hit me when I was forty," Jason said to Billie.

"I guess you take drugs for the pain," Billie said. "I hear they've got some good drugs now."

Ada looked down at the album in her lap. In the album there were children and babies and couples. Some of the couples had children next to them. Ada stared at the photos. Many of the faces were young, then you turned a page and the same faces were old. Esther seemed to remember everyone in the album. But she still didn't remember Ada. She was talking to Ada as to a friend, but Ada felt as if the ghost of her old self hovered in her mind waiting for a sign from Esther so that she could step forward again and be recognized.

"But that wouldn't interest you," Esther was saying as she flipped a page. Suddenly she shut the book and gazed intently at Ada.

"I don't know who you are," Esther said. "But I like you. Why don't you stay the night?" Ada looked over at Billie, who'd heard the invitation.

"Go ahead, Mother," Billie said, a little too eagerly. "I

can come for you tomorrow around two o'clock, after the luncheon.''

Ada looked at Jason, who was staring out the picture window toward the Mercedes. Maybe she should just give up on getting Esther to remember her and go back to the hotel and watch TV. But the moment she thought this, something unyielding rose up in her. She was determined to discover some moment when her image would suddenly appear before Esther from that lost time. Only then could they be together again as the friends they had once been, and that was what she had come for.

"You'll have to bring my things in from the car," Ada said at last.

"I wish I could help," Jason said to Billie, "but I can't. Fact is, I got to go and lay down again," he said to the room at large. Then he turned and moved slowly down the hallway. Billie opened the door and went out to the car. In a minute she came back with Ada's overnight bag.

"Have a nice time, Mom," she said. "I mean that." She set the bag inside the door. "I'll see you tomorrow." Ada knew she was glad to be heading back to the world of buying and selling, of tax shelters and the multiple uses of the llama. In a minute she heard Billie start up the Mercedes and heard it leave the drive.

The room seemed sparsely furnished now that she and Esther were alone. She could see a table leg just inside the door of a room that was probably the dining room. On the far wall was a large picture of an autumn landscape done in gold and brown.

"Look around, why don't you," Esther said, and raised herself off the couch. "It's a miracle, but I own this house."

They walked into the kitchen. The counter space was taken up with canned goods, stacks of dishes of every kind, and things Ada wouldn't expect to find in a kitchen

—things like gallon cans of paint. It was as if someone were afraid they wouldn't be able to get to a store and had laid in extra supplies of everything.

"I do the cooking," Esther said. "Everything's frozen but some wieners. Are wieners okay?"

"Oh, yes," Ada said. "But I'm not hungry just yet."

"I'm not either," Esther said. "I was just thinking ahead because I've got to put these feet up. Come back to the bedroom with me."

Ada thought this an odd suggestion, but she followed Esther down the hallway to a room with a rumpled bed and a chrome kitchen chair near the foot of the bed. There was a dresser with some medicine containers on it. Ada helped Esther get settled on the bed. She took one of the pillows and placed it under Esther's legs at the ankles. She was glad she could do this for her. But then she didn't know what to do next, or what to say. She wanted the past and not this person for whom she was just an interesting stranger. Ada sat down in the chair and looked at Esther.

"What ever became of Georgie Ganz and Florita White?" she asked Esther, because she had to say something.

"Ada—that's your name, isn't it? Ada, I don't know who you're talking about," Esther said. "I wish I did, but I don't."

"That's all right," Ada said. She brightened a little. It made her feel better that Georgie and Florita had also been forgotten. A shadow cast by the house next door had fallen into the room. Ada thought the sun must be going down. She felt she ought to be doing something, changing the course of events for her friend in some small but important way.

"Let me rub your feet," Ada said suddenly and raised herself from the chair. "Okay?" She moved over to the bed and began to massage Esther's feet.

"That feels good, honey," Esther said. "I haven't had anybody do that for me in years."

"Reminds me of that almond cream we used to rub on each other's feet after we'd served at a party all night," Ada said. The feet seemed feverish to her fingers. She saw that the veins were enlarged and angry-looking as she eased her hands over an ankle and up onto the leg.

After a little while, Esther said, "Honey, why don't you lie down with me on the bed. That way we can really talk."

At first Ada couldn't comprehend what Esther had said to her. She said she didn't mind rubbing Esther's feet. She said she wasn't tired enough to lie down. But Esther insisted.

"We can talk better that way," Esther said. "Come lay down beside me."

Ada realized she still had on her coat. She took it off and put it over the back of the chair. Then she took off her shoes and went to lie down next to Esther.

"Now this is better, isn't it?" Esther said, when Ada was settled. She patted Ada's hand. "I can close my eyes now and rest." In a minute, she closed her eyes. And then they began to talk.

"Do you know about that preacher who was sweet on me back in Mansfield?" Esther asked. Ada thought for a minute and then remembered and said she did. "I didn't tell that to too many, I feel sure," Esther said. This admission caused Ada to feel for a moment that her friend knew she was someone special. There was that, at least. Ada realized she'd been holding her breath. She relaxed a little and felt a current of satisfaction, something just short of recognition, pass between them.

"I must have told you all my secrets," Esther said quietly, her eyes still closed.

"You did!" Ada said, rising up a little. "We used to tell each other everything."

"Everything," Esther said, as if she were sinking into a place of agreement where remembering and forgetting didn't matter. Then there was a loud noise from the hall, and the sound of male voices at the door. Finally the front door closed, and Esther put her arm across Ada's arm and sighed.

"Good. He's gone," Esther said. "I wait all day for them to come and take him away. His friends, so called. He'll come home drunk, and he won't have a dime. They've all got nothing better to do."

"That must be an awful worry," Ada said. "It must be a heartache."

"Heartache?" Esther said, and then she made a weary sound. "You don't know the start of it, honey. 'You need me, Mom,' he says to me, 'and I need you.' I told him if he stopped drinking I'd will him my house so he'd always have a place to live. But he won't stop. I know he won't. He can't.

"You know what he did?" Esther asked and raised up a little on her pillow. "He just looked at me when I said that about willing him the house. I don't think he'd realized until then that I wasn't always going to be here," Esther said. "Poor fellow, he can't help himself. But girl, he'd drink it up if I left it to him."

Ada felt that the past had drifted away, and she couldn't think how to get back to that carefree time in Springfield. "It's a shame," she murmured. And then she thought of something to tell Esther that she hadn't admitted to anyone. "My husband nearly drank us out of house and home, too. He would have if I hadn't fought him tooth and nail. It's been five years since he died. Five peaceful years." She was relieved to hear herself admit this, but somehow ashamed too.

"Well, I haven't made it to the peaceful part yet," Esther said. "Jason has always lived with me. He'll never leave me. Where could he go?"

"He doesn't abuse you, does he?" Ada said. *Abuse* was a word she'd heard on the television and radio a lot these days, and it seemed all-purpose enough not to offend Esther.

"If you mean does he hit me, no he doesn't," Esther said. "But I sorrow over him. I do."

Ada had done her share of sorrowing too. She closed her eyes and let her hand rest on Esther's arm. Neither of them said anything for a while. The house was still. She caught the faint medicinal smell of ointment and rubbing alcohol. She wished she could say something to ease what Esther had to bear, but she couldn't think of anything that didn't sound like what Billie might call "sappy."

"What's going to become of Jason?" Ada said finally. But when she asked this she was really thinking of herself and of her friend.

"I'm not going to know," Esther said. "Memory's going to fall entirely away from me when I die, and I'm going to be spared that." She seemed, Ada thought, to be actually looking forward to death and the shutting down of all memory. Ada was startled by this admission.

Esther got up from the bed. "Don't mind me, honey. You stay comfortable. I have to go to the bathroom. It's these water pills."

After Esther left the room Ada raised up in bed as if she had awakened from the labyrinth of a strange dream. What was she doing here, she wondered, on this woman's bed in a city far from her own home? What business of hers was this woman's troubles? In Springfield, Esther had always told Ada how pretty she was and what beautiful hair she had, how nicely it took a wave. They had tried on each other's clothes and shared letters from home. But this was something else. This was the future and she had come here alone. There was no one to whom she could turn and say without the least vanity, "I was pretty, wasn't I?" She sat on the side of the bed and waited for the moment to pass. But it was like an echo that wouldn't stop calling her. Then she heard from outside the house the merry, untroubled laughter of some girls. It must be dark out by now, she thought. It must be night. She got up from the bed, went to the window and pulled back the sheet that served as a curtain. A car was pulling away from the house next door. The lights brushed the room as it moved past. In a moment, she went back to the bed and lay down again.

For supper Esther gave her wieners, and green beans fixed the way they'd had them back home, with bacon drippings. Then she took her to the spare room, which was next to Jason's room. They had to move some boxes off the bed. Esther fluffed up the pillows and put down an extra blanket. Then she moved over to the doorway.

"If you need anything, if you have any bad dreams, you just call me, honey," she said. "Sometimes I dream I'm wearing a dress but it's on backwards and I'm coming downstairs, and there's a whole room full of people looking up at me," she said. "I'm glad you're here. I am. Good night. Good night, Ada."

"Good night, Esther," Ada said. But Esther went on standing there in the doorway.

Ada looked at her and wished she could dream them both back to a calm summer night in Springfield. She would open her window and call across the alley to her friend, "You awake?" and Esther would hear her and come to the screen and they would say wild and hopeless things like, Why don't we go to California and try out for the movies? Crazy things like that. But Ada didn't remind Esther of this. She lay there alone in their past and looked at Esther, at her old face and her old hands coming out of the sleeves of her robe, and she wanted to yell at her to get out, shut the door, don't come back! She hadn't come here to strike up a friendship with this old scarecrow of a woman. But then Esther did something. She came over to the bed and pulled the covers over Ada's shoulders and patted her cheek.

"There now, dear," she said. "I'm just down the hall if you need me." And then she turned and went out of the room.

Sometime before daylight Ada heard a scraping sound in the hall. Then something fell loudly to the floor. But in a while the scraping sound started again and someone entered the room next to hers and shut the door. It was Jason, she supposed. Jason had come home, and he was drunk and only a few feet away. She had seen her own husband like this plenty of times, had felt herself forgotten, obliterated, time after time. She lay there rigid and felt the weight of the covers against her throat. Suddenly, it was as if she were suffocating. She felt her mouth open and a name came out of it. "Esther! Esther!" she cried. And in a few moments her door opened and her friend came in and leaned over her.

"What is it, honey?" Esther said, and turned the lamp on next to the bed.

"I'm afraid," Ada said, and she put out her hand and took hold of Esther's sleeve. "Don't leave," she said. Esther waited a minute. Then she turned off the light and got into bed beside Ada. Ada turned on her side, facing the wall, and Esther's arm went around her shoulder.

The next day Billie came to the house a little early. Ada had just finished helping Esther wash her hair.

"I want you to take some pictures of us," Ada said to Billie. "Esther and me." She dug into her purse and took out the Kodak she'd carried for just this purpose. Billie seemed in a hurry to get on the road now that the conference was over.

"I was a real hit last night," Billie said to Ada as if she'd missed seeing her daughter at her best. Little tufts of llama wool clung to Billie's suit jacket as she took the camera from Ada and tried to figure out where the lens was and how to snap the picture. Ada felt sure she hadn't missed anything, but she understood Billie's wanting her to know she'd done well at something. That made sense to her now.

"Let's go out in the yard," Billie said.

"My hair's still wet," Esther said. She was standing in front of a mirror near the kitchen rubbing her hair with a towel, but the hair sprang out in tight spirals all over her head.

"You look all right," Ada said. "You look fine, honey."

"You'd say anything to make a girl feel good," Esther said.

"No, I wouldn't," Ada said. She stood behind Esther and, looking in the mirror, dabbed her own nose with powder. They could be two young women readying themselves to go out, Ada thought. They might meet some young men while they were out, and they might not. In any case, they'd take each other's arm and stroll until dusk. Someone—Ada didn't know who—might pass and admire them.

Billie had them stand in front of the picture window. They put their arms around each other. Esther was shorter and leaned her head onto Ada's shoulder. She even smiled. Ada had the sensation that the picture had already been taken somewhere in her past. She was sure it had.

"Did you get it?" Ada said as Billie advanced the film and moved closer for another shot.

"I'm just covering myself," Billie said, squatting down on the lawn and aiming the camera like a professional. "You'll kill me if these don't turn out." She snapped a few more shots from the driveway, then handed the camera back to her mother.

Ada followed her friend into the house to collect her belongings and say goodbye. Esther wrapped a towel around her head while Ada gathered her coat, purse, and overnight bag.

"Honey, I'm so sorry I never remembered you," Esther said.

Ada believed Esther when she said this. *Sorry* was the word a person had to use when there was no way to change a situation. Still, she wished they could have changed it.

"I remembered *you*, that's the main thing," Ada said. But a miserable feeling came over her, and it was all she could do to speak. Somehow the kindness and intimacy they'd shared as girls had lived on in them. But Esther, no matter how much she might want to, couldn't remember Ada, and give it back to her, except as a stranger.

"God, kid, I hate to see you go," Esther said. Her eyes filled. It seemed to Ada that they might both be wiped from the face of the earth by this parting. They embraced and clung to each other a moment. Ada patted Esther's thin back, and then moved hurriedly toward the door.

"Tell me all about your night," Billie said, as Ada slid into the passenger's seat. But Ada knew this was really the last thing on Billie's mind. And anyhow, it all seemed so far from anything Ada had ever experienced that she didn't know where to begin.

"Honey, I just want to be still for a while," Ada said. She didn't care whether Billie smoked or how fast she drove. She knew that eventually she would tell Billie how she had tried to make Esther remember her, and how she had failed. But the important things—the way Esther had come to her when she'd called out, and how, earlier, they'd lain side by side—this would be hers. She wouldn't say anything to Billy about these things. She couldn't. She doubted she ever would. She looked out at the countryside that flew past the window in a green blur. It went on and on, a wall of forest that crowded the edge of the roadway. Then there was a gap in the color and she found herself looking at downed trees and stumps where an entire hillside of forest had been cut away. Her hand went to her face as if she had been slapped. But then she saw it was green again, and she let her hand drop to her lap.